LIVE ❤ LIFE
A B E R D E E N S H I R E

livelifeaberdeenshire.org.uk/libraries

While the events described and some of the characters in these twelve stories may be based on actual historical events and real people, in reference to the BCA's oral archives, the characters created by the authors are fictional and their stories are a work of fiction.

Published in the UK by Scholastic, 2021
Euston House, 24 Eversholt Street, London, NW1 1DB
Scholastic Ireland, 89E Lagan Road, Dublin Industrial Estate, Glasnevin, Dublin, D11 HP5F

SCHOLASTIC and associated logos are trademarks and/or
registered trademarks of Scholastic Inc.

Foreword © Baroness Floella Benjamin, DBE, 2021
Fact files by K.N. Chimbiri © Scholastic, 2021
'Not Made From Around Here' © Ashley Hickson-Lovence, 2021
'A Letter Home' and 'The Wind and the Snow' © E.L. Norry, 2021
'Mountain Side' and 'Green Angel' © Judy Hepburn, 2021
'Eliza King is at Home' and 'Making Friends the British Way: Lucille's Story' © Katy Massey, 2021
'Diary of a Windrush Kid' © Jermain Jackman, 2021
'A Night in London' © Kirsty Latoya, 2021
'The Light at the End of the Tunnel' © Kevin George, 2021
'Hale and Hearty' © Salena Godden, 2021
'Made to Measure' © Quincy the Comedian, 2021

Cover illustration by Joelle Avelino

For picture credits see page 141. Every effort has been made to ensure that this information is correct at the time of
going to print. Any errors will be corrected upon reprint.

ISBN 978 07023 0790 4

A CIP catalogue record for this book is available from the British Library.

Printed in Italy by Elcograf S.p.A.
Paper made from wood grown in sustainable forests and other controlled sources.

1 3 5 7 9 10 8 6 4 2

www.scholastic.co.uk

THE PLACE FOR ME
STORIES ABOUT THE
WINDRUSH
GENERATION

Fact files by **K.N. Chimbiri**
Stories by **Kevin George**, **Salena Godden**, **Judy Hepburn**,
Ashley Hickson-Lovence, **Jermain Jackman**, **Kirsty Latoya**, **Katy Massey**,
E.L. Norry and **Quincy the Comedian**

SCHOLASTIC

CONTENTS

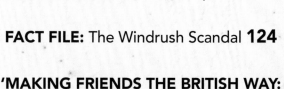

FOREWORD BY
DAME FLOELLA BENJAMIN

On 1 September 1960, aged ten, I arrived with three of my siblings to a cold and unwelcoming Britain after making the 6,400-kilometre (4000-mile) voyage from Trinidad. My parents had arrived eighteen months earlier with my two younger siblings to set up home before sending for us. It seems amazing in this day and age that four small children could make a journey unaccompanied on a passenger ship.

I was so excited as we docked in Southampton and even the freezing rain didn't dampen my spirits as I made my way down the gangplank, dressed up in my pretty dress, my hair in neat ribbons.

My joy wasn't to last long as I realized I was going to be treated as a colour and not as a person. At school we were relentlessly bullied; only the sanctuary of the one room all eight of us shared kept me going.

At school in Trinidad I had been taught all about Britain, about its heroes, its poets and its history. I was told the Queen loved me and that I was British! Every day we sang 'God Save the Queen' in the schoolyard, before going into school. I wasn't taught anything about the history of my people, about how we came to be in the Caribbean. How for centuries thousands upon thousands of African people were transported from their homeland as enslaved people. They were treated mercilessly, their culture and identity torn from them as they toiled to make Britain prosperous. But as a child, I didn't know all this and going to Britain was equivalent of going to Disneyland – I was going to see the Queen!

My father, like many Caribbeans, had decided to seek work and a new life in Britain, following in the footsteps of the 1948 Windrush pioneers, who had answered the call to come to Britain to rebuild the country after the Second World War. Adverts had appeared in Caribbean newspapers inviting people to travel to Britain.

However, the welcome they received was not what they expected. To quote one pioneer, "We could not get on a bus and go back home..."

The people came with hope and optimism in their hearts, not only searching for a new life, but with a real sense of duty to what they, like myself, believed to be the Motherland, the Land of Hope and Glory, Mother of the Free.

They were treated abominably in many ways, which was partly due to the lack of information put out by the government of the day, explaining why Caribbean people were arriving in Britain. The most poignant memory many new arrivals had from searching for accommodation was the signs saying 'No Coloureds, No Irish, No dogs'.

Despite all this, the Windrush generation was instrumental in building the National Health Service (NHS) and the railways, and generally putting Britain back on its feet. Over the following decades they worked tirelessly, often at the expense of their own families; mothers and fathers often too tired to dedicate quality time to home life.

Until recently very few of the Windrush generation spoke openly about their experiences and shared the trials and tribulations they went through. Then suddenly many found themselves embroiled in the almost unbelievable situation of being threatened with deportation unless they could prove their immigration status. But because of this 'Windrush Scandal' many British people are beginning to have empathy and understanding for the incredible resilience, determination, dignity and dedication the Windrush generation showed in the face of adversity and rejection. Black Lives Matter has also shone a spotlight on the injustice and prejudice faced by Black people, not just in the UK but across the world.

But we must not let hatred and resentment define us. We must create diversity nirvana, for the sake of our descendants and those who follow us – our children. We need to know all our history before we turn our faces to the future because that's where our destiny lies.

I want the 2020s to be the new age of enlightenment, as we face global problems that affect us all, because all life matters. So we must strive to ensure that in future decades when people look back at this time, they will say that's when the wrongs were righted … when the shackles were broken and eyes were opened.

I am proud to Chair the Windrush Commemoration Committee, charged with commissioning a significant and permanent national monument to celebrate the enormous contribution made to Britain by the Windrush generation.

BLACK CULTURAL ARCHIVES

INTRODUCTION

Black Cultural Archives, as home to Black British history, is immensely proud to present this collection of stories about the Windrush generation, members of whom were the pioneering force behind the founding of our archive and heritage centre.

Long before BCA opened its doors to the public, founder Len Garrison established the African-Caribbean Education Resource, to give Black children opportunities to learn their history and culture, and to excel academically. Thus, BCA's commitment to improving educational outcomes was, and remains, a cornerstone of our vision.

The Place for Me: Stories about the Windrush Generation is our first publishing collaboration, and we look forward to sharing more of our histories through literature so that people of all colours and backgrounds can learn about Britain's rich history – its mistakes and failures as well as its glories and triumphs, because it is only with a clear vision of the past that we can move forward and build a strong society.

BCA is grateful to the people of the Windrush generation, honoured to record their stories, humbled by their sacrifices, and supportive of their ongoing challenges.

Overall, we hope these rich and moving stories of the past will be enjoyed by many readers.

Black Cultural Archives,
Brixton, London

NOT MADE FROM AROUND HERE

ASHLEY HICKSON-LOVENCE

Al is at home as usual, flicking through the channels, hoping something might catch his eye. His knees aren't so good these days and he hasn't yet built up the courage to climb the stairs to go to bed; he knows it will hurt. He flicks past a quiz show and then the news (which he has already watched twice today) and then a documentary about the ice caps melting, before stopping when he briefly sees a shot of a street in West London he vaguely recognizes. Just as he racks his brain trying to remember this semi-familiar street, the shot disappears, and then two young women with long brunette hair are speaking in posh voices about a skiing holiday or something. After a few minutes, with one of the women now annoyed by the bitter taste of her fancy coffee, the camera again shows a part of West London Al definitely knows, but it looks very different to when he first arrived in the city back in 1958.

He continues watching, not really understanding what's going on or who the Jonty, Barnaby or Montague they are talking about are, but hoping to spot more shots of the streets that he used to wander through as a young man. He leans forward and squints. Even with his glasses on, his eyes aren't as good as they used to be. After a few more minutes of the posh women talking, they show another quick shot of his old road. If the camera panned out just a little more, Al is sure he would be able to see the little flat he rented soon after he reached the UK.

An advert about a new hybrid car is now playing, but whatever that programme was before has got Al thinking about how life used to be when he first arrived in this country. He remembers he couldn't wait to come to the mother country and see how the other half lived.

The boat took three weeks to arrive in Dover, but he didn't mind, he had all the food and drink in the world. The big boat even had a cinema. When he reached England, he took a train to London Victoria before his friend picked him up and took Al to stay with him in Fulham Palace Road. Al remembers how the cold weather went right through the skin and into the bones in those first few days.

Back then, in the late 1950s, he and six others were living in one room, all good people from all over the Caribbean: Jamaica, Guyana, St Lucia and Trinidad. His good good friends were Marcy and Sam, a married couple from the same place Al was from – the island of Grenada.

Grenada is sometimes called the Isle of Spice, but as Al boarded the bus home from work one chilly evening, he felt far from spicy, trembling like a leaf in hurricane season. Al had finished his nine-hour shift washing dishes in a hotel in Green Park, with the one pound he had earned for a day's work in his pocket. He was in good spirits, humming a little calypso tune from back home and looking forward to playing a game of cards and maybe some dominoes back in the flat. He hopped off the bus a few stops early to go to the shop first. Working all day had made him thirsty, so he would need a couple of cans to wet his whistle a bit.

For most Black people, there were three things to be wary of living in West London at the time: the cold, the police (depending on which officers were on duty) and the Teddy Boys. Every Black person was on edge because of the Teddy Boys, after what happened at the Notting Hill Riots a few months before, but Al was a confident twenty-year-old, he wasn't scared to go walking around Hammersmith, West Brompton, Fulham, Chelsea or West Kensington. As far as he was concerned, London was his new home, what was there to be afraid of?

The Teddy Boys were far from cuddly. They would roam the streets in large packs, like a rugby team, and didn't like people like Al or his friends simply because they had darker skin than they did. They didn't like people who looked different, ate different kinds of food and listened to different kinds of music. They had a special uniform: big boots with the laces done up tight to the top, super tight jeans and tall spiky hair. They were young boys really, aged fifteen to twenty-five, but they could be ferocious when they fancied a fight. It was true that most of the older people around there didn't like people like Al and other Black people either, but unlike the Teddy Boys they said it with their eyes, not their fists. A few nights before, he was speaking with Marcy and Sam about them over the chicken pie Marcy had baked for dinner.

"You've got to be careful out there you know, Al," Marcy said with worry in her voice.

"Careful of who?" Al replied, knowing already exactly who she was talking about.

"Them Teddy Boys are running riot out there, you know."

"They wouldn't dare touch me, look how strong I am," Al said, tensing his non-existent muscles.

"You think I'm joking, just last week them hoodlums throw stones at me while I was in the phone box on the corner of Sherlin Road. The whole glass was in splinters, five minutes more and it would have completely shattered over me like hailstones."

"Me good Marcy, trust me, sticks and stones can't break my bones.

If they throw stones, me throw rocks," Al said and laughed.

"You have nothing to say to him, Sam?" Marcy asked, jutting her head towards Sam, who was busy enjoying his food. After a few ungraceful chews, Sam wiped the corners of his mouth clean with a napkin and looked at Al.

"All I will say is this, if you're not careful, one of these days, you're going to get seriously hurt." And then he quickly shoved another spoonful of pie in his mouth.

Marcy was a bright woman but she was wrong about this. This was Al's new home and he thought being scared of some young men in tight pants and gelled hair was stupid.

Later that evening, Al turned the corner towards the little shop near the flat, whistling away with a spring in his step. Then, almost like a shadow that wasn't his, he felt a strange presence suddenly behind him.

"Who've we got here then?" a tall Teddy Boy said, stepping in front of Al from a little alleyway on the left. With one in front and six or seven behind, Al suddenly realized he was completely surrounded.

He tried to stay calm even though his heart was beating fast, sending tremors all over his body.

"Got a cigarette, mate?" the ringleader asked. His teeth were all crooked and yellow.

When Al looked down, he could see just how heavy their boots looked, he imagined how painful it would be if – probably when – the boots made contact with his head. He tried not to speak – if they hadn't guessed already, they would know immediately that he was a West Indian if he did.

"Did you not hear me?" the Teddy Boy asked, grabbing Al by the scruff of his neck. His hair was taller and spikier than the other boys' which is probably why he was the leader. Al cleared his throat and tried to put on his best British accent.

"Me, sir, smoke? Oh no, certainly not, sir." It hadn't worked. The posh fake accent only seemed to make the Teddy Boy angrier. Al could see that his right fist was red and clenched so Al closed his eyes and waited for the first hit.

But right then, just in the nick of time, Al opened his eyes to see Marcy and Sam coming down the road. Marcy was waving a wooden rolling pin in the air angrily like the women back in the fields used to do to scare the birds away from their crops. She and Sam must have been worried why Al wasn't home yet and come looking for him. Al could see in the faces of the Teddy Boys that they were more scared of Marcy and her rolling pin than Sam. She was a big woman, Marcy, but clearly nimble on her feet as she approached Al and the Teddy Boys at speed. The ringleader's grip around Al's shirt collar quickly loosened, and before Al had even started dusting himself down, they were gone, off down the road, around the corner and out of sight.

"Why did you do that for?" Al asked, straightening his tie, apparently annoyed they had intervened. "I had them right where I wanted them…"

"Of course you did, Al, of course you did," said Sam, putting his arm over his shoulder and leading him back to the flat.

"I did!" Al exclaimed, knowing they didn't believe him.

I wouldn't have believed me either, old Al thinks, as he flicks off the TV, rises to his feet slowly and begins to hobble up the stairs to bed.

Empire Windrush arriving at Tilbury Docks, Essex, 21 June 1948

Five young boxers and their manager arrive in the UK on board the *Empire Windrush*

FACT FILE

BEFORE THE ARRIVAL OF EMPIRE WINDRUSH

• •

In the past, Britain claimed many colonies around the world including countries in Africa and the Caribbean. Sometimes people, usually men, from those colonies came to Britain in small numbers. Often, they came alone to study or they came on ships working as seamen. Sometimes they decided to remain in Britain, occasionally marrying local white British women. Over time some small Black communities developed in areas like Cardiff, Liverpool and London's East End. The Black and mixed-race communities in Britain before the Second World War were usually working class although some people were middle class.

Before the Second World War most people in Britain never met or saw a Black person in real life. Most white British people only saw Black people in movies or in books. Racial discrimination was commonplace in Britain in those days so life was often difficult for the small numbers of Black people living there. Black people found it hard to get jobs and they were usually turned away from joining the armed forces because they were not white. They couldn't enter some hotels, pubs, restaurants and even churches because of their colour.

* * *

Dr Harold A. Moody was a civil rights activist. Harold came to Britain from Jamaica in 1904 to study medicine. Although he graduated at the top of his class, Harold was refused a position at any hospital because he was Black. So, Harold decided to set up his own private practice as a GP at his home in Peckham, South London. In those days there was no NHS and people had to

• •

pay to see a doctor. Harold often treated the children of working-class people for free. 'The Black Doctor' was well known in the area and he was popular.

Harold was very active in his church and later on, in 1931, he also set up an organization called the League of Coloured Peoples. This became Britain's most important organization to fight racism and help Black people with housing, education, jobs and racial justice.

Dr Harold A. Moody

ENGLISH HERITAGE
DR
HAROLD
MOODY
1882 ~ 1947
Campaigner
for Racial Equality
lived and worked
here

A plaque commemorating the life and work of Dr Moody, erected in 1995

A LETTER HOME

NOVEMBER, 1958

E.L. NORRY

My dear sister,

Well, no sharks gobbled me up and I didn't fall overboard neither! I'm here, finally: England. The 'mother country' we learned so much about at school. Remember all our whispers of princes and high tea, castles and *Alice in Wonderland*? Huddled under the covers, during our endless summers and rainy seasons, giggling as girls? Seems a lifetime ago.

"What's it like?" I can imagine the fire sparking in your eyes as you ask. I can tell you, I've found no streets paved with gold. No Wonderland here. No beautiful manor houses: rather, cramped houses like little boxes, squashed so tight that the poor sky barely gets a look in!

My heart still beats with you – thousands of miles away – but it feels right, to be here with Eric. He drives the Tube and although he's deep underground, and his skin is looking too chalky, he's almost back to his old self, now that he's working again. Smiling and laughing like when he worked on the plantation. I think he just needed to feel useful, you know? He works long hours but earns sixteen shillings a week – can you imagine!

Where to begin? On the boat, I met a nice lady going off to be a medical secretary in Manchester; not our Manchester but the one here in England. She told me the country is desperate for nurses, so I'm hoping to start training for the NHS. It's an amazing service and offers free healthcare to everyone. Truly a miracle.

I was bone-chillingly freezing stepping off that gangplank, surprised to see my own breath misting around me like an apparition. I struggled with my suitcase, bulging with my hopes and dreams, fretting because my suit was creased. The cold was like a slap and my arms practically turned purple! Months later and I'm still not used to it. But Eric was there, waiting for me, and he had a big coat to wrap me in. A heavy, scratchy wool thing, but with his arms tight around me, I barely noticed.

I want to be honest about what life is like here, but whatever I tell you, there's no need to worry. You know I can always take care of myself and I have Eric too. But still, don't say too much of this to our friends and neighbours because I'm not sure they'll understand. As you know, my sense of humour is my guiding light; it keeps me smiling, even though at times my heart feels blacker than the night, with no stars to be seen. I can't tell you how many times I thank the Lord and count our blessings.

The weather itself seems against us though. How it messes with my hair; oh Lord! Wind, sleet, rain – not rain like we know: warm, and soon dried up, sizzling on the concrete, but bitter, little needles of spite, driving themselves into my skin. Where is the sun? I miss the lilies and orchids, swinging palms and the whispers of the sugar cane waving in the breeze…

At the moment, I work in a nursery looking after white babies. I spend so long indoors that my dreams are filled with rolling hills and colours like you wouldn't believe; always dreams of home. Them babies sure do cry a lot, squished red faces. One or two white women I work with are nice enough, though the other day I heard one say the babies were scared of 'us darkies'. Stupid!

Sometimes they whisper and then the talking stops when I walk in. Little looks, hurts hidden; as if we wouldn't notice. As if we can't feel it in the air. Yesterday, a lady in the shop got served before me, even though I was there first. I waited for her to say something, but no. So I just waited, quiet. Making a fuss isn't the way to get heard. Our time will come. I repeat Galatians 6:9: *Let us not become weary in doing good, for at the proper time we will reap a harvest if we do not give up.*

I want to build something of our life over here: have a career, make my time on God's good Earth really count. But sister – they sure want our sugar and bananas more than they want us.

The skies are greyer than anything else. Smoke belches out of chimneys and the views feel small and grey too. No sorrel trees in sight. No macaws or hummingbirds, only grey pigeons. Grey, grey, grey – how many shades of the same dullness can there be?

But, you know me … if you look, there is always sunshine to be found. So I make sure I notice, on those rare days when the sun does peek out, that those pigeons' feathers have a vibrant rainbow sheen. And when it rains, if the light catches the drops just right, then they sparkle on the pavement. I make believe they're diamonds; that this place has unseen glittering jewels. We just need to search for them.

I'm trying to hold on to the idea that we made the correct decision. Telling myself all the time, how important it is to earn money, send it back home, provide for everyone, but sister, sadly, it might be a long time before us island folk are seen as equals.

Life is now so different! The strangest thing? Folks not talking to, or even looking at, each other on the street. No one smiles. That would never happen back home. We say "Morning" and "Hello": being polite, having good manners. But here, people keep themselves to themselves. How anyone gets to know anyone else, I really don't know.

After a long time looking, we found a place to live. It's not home yet, but I'm working on it. The boarding house is split up into different rooms; lots of other West Indians here. Doors slam and bang all times of day and night, but we're slowly getting to know the others. We boil water and bring it into our little room to wash. Not allowed a radio or a fridge – they'd use up too much electricity and raise the rent, so we put things on the windowsill if we need them cold. We all share one cooker in the hallway and that shared cooker leads to some conversations, I can tell you! But the smells remind me of home.

How's the pastor? I dressed up last Sunday and went to the nearest church on my own because Eric was working overtime. When I started singing, I felt eyes on me the whole time. Maybe I lifted up my voice too loud? I stayed though – wanted to give thanks. But the praise didn't feel like any sort of celebration. Afterwards, the vicar stopped me on my way out. He said, politely, almost a whisper, "Thank you so much for coming, but I'd appreciate it if you never come back again." Me ears couldn't believe it. Him supposed to be a man of God! My heart nearly broke, but then I got to thinking… God would never agree with people being told they can't celebrate his name. So on the way home I stopped those tears and just repeated Isaiah 41:10 under my breath.

I never told Eric though, couldn't bring myself to speak of it. The shame weighed me down. I'll ask the people who live upstairs what they do on Sundays; maybe we should make our own churches.

They like to focus on difference. They have these signs up in shops, and in windows: no coloureds, no Irish, no dogs, no children. I ask you – what colour do I look like? How quickly they've forgotten our men fighting with them against Hitler.

A few months ago, in the summer, near where we live in Notting Hill, there was terrible fighting. The phone box at the end of our road was smashed up, glass all over. Two hundred in the streets – it made the newspapers and TV. 'Riots' they said, but they were attacks on our Black men. Eric says no man feels safe walking alone at night, so they stick together – and it seems some don't like that.

Shops, windows and homes were destroyed. Some young men here wear big heavy boots and grease back their hair – call themselves 'Teddy Boys', but there ain't nothing cuddly or soft about them! Fear stamped across their faces like their acne. Spouting rubbish about 'Keeping Britain White', wanting to stir up trouble; unwilling to open their hearts or minds. Warning the men to keep away from 'their women'. As if any woman wants a bully for a husband.

But still … it's best if you don't come over so soon; wait a while. Things will soon quiet down, madness like this can't last. Thankfully, justice come: nine white boys got sentenced to four years in prison, they were the ones who started it. Maybe things are stirring, changing. I pray – hope – it'll be different for our children. Eric and I want to start a family soon. Freedom and companionship will come again.

Small pleasures can be found: the markets, dominoes, music, even if the air is too thick and the sky too small. We'll save up and have our own house, one day. Got to look forward. As Jeremiah 29:11 tells us: *plans to prosper us, not to harm.*

Yes, I miss the sunlight, the warmth, the bustle of community, the ease of … just being. But tonight, we have plans! Earlier, Eric went to get us fish and chips for our Friday dinner. He got talking to a couple from Barbados who've been here five years; they invited us round to have a drink and listen to music. For the first time in months, I'm excited. And I believe deep in my heart that the next time I write, my news will be brighter, just like how the sunshine back home dances on the water. I'll be dancing soon enough.

God bless and all my love,

Gloria xxx

FIRST BLACK CULTURAL ARCHIVES MUSEUM IN BRITAIN

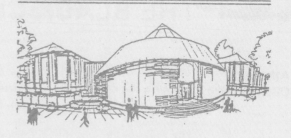

'The past is what all people build their present and future on; without this they sit in a void waiting to reclaim their history, suspended in a bottomless pit.'

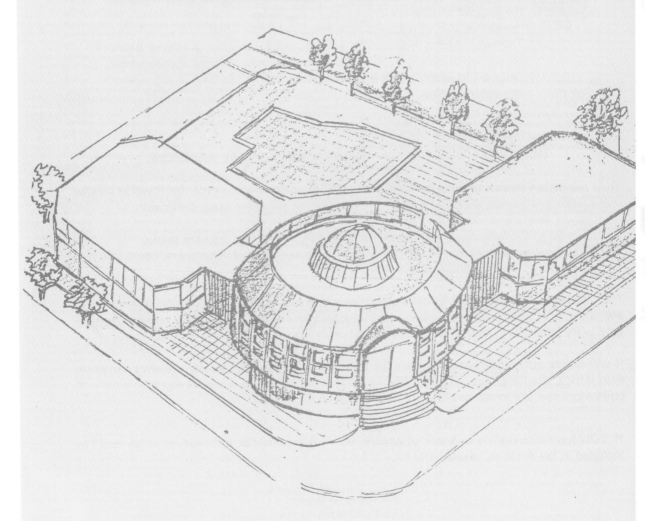

THE AFRICAN PEOPLES HISTORICAL MONUMENT FOUNDATION (UK)

THE BLACK CULTURAL ARCHIVES
COLDHARBOUR WORKS, COLDHARBOUR LANE, LONDON SW9 8RR
Tel: 274 7700

Supporters picketing Lambeth Town Hall for use of the Somerleyton Road site by Black Cultural Archives.

Left: Black Cultural Archives had their first official building on the corner of Coldharbour Lane and Atlantic Road in Brixton from 1985. They continuously campaigned for funding for a new heritage centre which was due to be built on Somerleyton Road as part of a larger building complex.

FACT FILE

THE SECOND WORLD WAR

- -

During the Second World War more white British people began to meet Black people in real life for the first time. Thousands of Black people from Britain's colonies, mainly men, came to help Britain during the war. Some came from the Caribbean, others from Africa. Later on when the USA joined the war, more than 130,000 African American men came to Britain too. After the war ended most of the Black servicemen gradually left Britain.

In 1948 a British ship called the *Empire Windrush* brought around a thousand people from the Caribbean to Britain. Some of the men who travelled on the *Empire Windrush* from the Caribbean to London in 1948 were ex-servicemen. They returned to the Caribbean after the war but conditions there were not good so they decided to return to Britain. Britain needed rebuilding after the war and there were many jobs available for people who wanted to work.

It was three years after the end of the war and many white British people were unhappy about the *Empire Windrush* bringing Black people from the Caribbean to live in Britain.

The *Empire Windrush* was not the first ship to bring Caribbean people to Britain after the war. In 1947 two ships, the *Ormonde* and the *Almanzora*, brought hundreds of Caribbean ex-servicemen to Britain.

After the *Empire Windrush*, more Caribbean people came to Britain on different ships and later on by plane. By 1971 about 500,000 people from

- -

the Caribbean had come to Britain. Although most of these people didn't travel on the *Empire Windrush* and came up to more than twenty years later, we call all these settlers the 'Windrush generation'.

The Windrush generation came to Britain for many reasons: some had been promised jobs; others wanted to find jobs after they arrived. Some wanted to study. Some were in the Royal Air Force and they were just returning from leave as although the war had ended not everyone had left the armed forces yet.

Many of them were invited to work for the NHS, London Transport, and other companies.

Above: some of the passengers of the *Empire Windrush*

Right: the ex-troopship *Empire Windrush* arriving at Tilbury Docks

MOUNTAIN SIDE

JUDY HEPBURN

Granny had a lot to do before she packed my grip. She washed and pressed my shirts, paired up socks and folded vests, spreading them out on her iron bedstead.

Now she lays them criss-cross in the suitcase. She does all this without speaking and I watch her silently.

When she snaps it shut I say, "Why you nuh come too, Granny?"

She doesn't answer. Her face doesn't change. I watch for a clue.

"Look here," she says after a while, "you slide this button across when you want to open it. See it here?" A metallic clasp springs open like a trap.

"Granny?" I ask again.

"Who go feed the fowl dem when you gone, eh?"

She shuts the case again and puts it on the floor; straightens the sheet.

"Anyway, Betty May travelling too, she go look after you. You 'member her?"

I nod. Betty May is older than me and I like her. She had been at school when I first started and now helps her parents in the shop down the road.

Tomorrow, I'm going to England on a big ship. My mother sent the money for my ticket. I haven't seen her for seven years, Granny says, since I was three and now I'm ten. I'm excited to see my mother but, well, I'd like for Granny to rub my back when I catch a cold.

The next morning, Granny blows on my face to wake me. It's dark and the oil lamp makes my shadow big on the wall as I put on my crisp white shirt and new long trousers.

She gives me two things when we say goodbye. One is some johnny cakes that she's made for the journey, and the other is a photograph taken a few years ago. We're standing at the side of the road, her and Grandpa and me. I hardly recognize us dressed up in our Sunday best.

I've been to Kingston once before. We got up in the dark then too and travelled in the back of an open-air truck in amongst all the ladies and their vegetables, on our way to Coronation Market. The air was cool as we breezed along the country roads, up Spur Tree Hill – where all the trees grow one way on account of the wind that always blows in the same direction – and then onwards towards the city. We got there at dawn. Soon the sun was blazing hot, not like the cooler mountain air of my home.

Coronation Market is a rowdy place with people calling out "Morning" to friends they haven't seen all week, unloading their produce – picked or cut only a few hours before – and setting up the stalls ready for their early customers.

This time Betty May and I are travelling in the cabin of the truck so we stay fresh. We get dropped off first, at the wharf. It's still at least a couple of hours until we'll be allowed on the ship. I spot it in the harbour alongside the wharf, its towering red-and-black funnel pumping out smoke already. RMS *Ascania* is written in white letters on its black hull. There's a smell of salty sea and tar and heat.

Betty May smiles down at me. "Someone making porridge. You want some?"

Soon I'm sitting in front of a nearby stall, an enamel bowl of steaming banana porridge on the table. I pick up my spoon.

"Mind you burn your tongue," she says.

We sit in heaven, spooning up little bits of cinnamon-sweet porridge, and blowing on it before slipping it into our mouths.

"Jamaicans always find a way to make a lickle money, eh?" a man at the next table is saying to a lady and two small girls, their hair in neat plaits. They look sad, like they've come to wave him goodbye.

Betty May and I stand in the queue at the bottom of the gangplank, about to board the ship.

"You ready? Must be our turn soon."

My hand tightens on my grip as we shuffle towards the looming hull that rises out of the water beside us. It bobs up and down and the gangplank wobbles to and fro, looking very small and narrow. I step on to it and, with one hand holding my suitcase, I only have the other to hold the rail and keep my balance as we travel skywards to the deck. Looking down into the swirling water makes me giddy. I stay as close to Betty May as I can and keep my eyes on her back. When we reach the top and step on to the deck I am feeling scared but victorious.

"You!"

I wonder who the ship's officer is talking to.

"You!" he says again and I realize with a jolt he's talking to me.

"You're too old to stay with the women. You're to bunk up with the men."

"But we're together," I hear Betty May protesting.

"He's too old. Move along!"

I get herded off with the men and see Betty May disappearing in another direction. "Don't worry," she calls back, though she looks worried herself.

"I'll find you in the dining room."

Tears spring up and I hold them down. This is what wearing long trousers brings. Suddenly I'm supposed to be a man but I'm a little boy all by myself on a big ship.

I follow the line down to the cabins. Each one holds ten bunk beds squashed up together and I'm given an underneath one. I put my grip at the bottom of the bed as I see the other men doing. Then I sit down on the side of the bed and wait. There are lots of legs and a lot of chit-chat as some of the men recognize each other.

A voice above me suddenly says, "Hey, you for Miss Palmer, nuh so?"

I look up. A familiar face, with a small moustache! It's Cecil, who I used to see sometimes in Santa Cruz when Granny took me down the mountain. He worked in Mr Myers' shop selling cloth and other dry goods. Mental arithmetic was his thing. Granny always worked out what three and a half yards at nine pence three farthings a yard was on a piece of paper before we got there, but he would do it in his head straight away and always got the same answer as Granny, she said.

"You travelling on your own? Who you here with?"

"Betty May," I say, trying hard not to have a shaky voice. "They separate us."

"Don't worry," he says. "I go look out for you."

And so Cecil takes me under his wing for all the time that the sea and sky turn from blue to grey and my clothes turn from short sleeves to winter jumpers. I have all my meals with Betty May and the friends she's made. Often, Cecil and his friends join us. He and Betty May like each other, I can tell.

"What you go do, Cecil, when you reach?" she asks him.

"I will find a job, don't you worry. Maybe a carpenter. I'm good at math and can work the wood. How about you?"

"I'm going to be a nurse. I got recruited."

Betty May is going to Birmingham, where she has an auntie, but Cecil doesn't even have an address. She gives him hers and he promises to write once he's settled.

We dock in Southampton and get on a train that has its rails right up close to the wharf. We travel to Waterloo Station in London. I stand with Betty May and wait, looking into the throng of people come to greet the passengers, wondering which one is my mother. At last, a lady stops in front of us.

"Hello," she says. "Is that you, Carl? I'm your mummy."

We look at each other. I don't know what I expected. I feel shy when she gives me a hug. Betty May wishes me luck, squeezing my hand tight. I squeeze hers back. She walks over to Cecil who is standing a few yards away and I watch him put his arm around her waist. They both turn and wave. I wave back, then turn to follow my mother out of the station.

When we get to the flat I notice she has the same photo Granny gave me of us standing at the side of the road. It's in a silver frame on the mantelpiece over the gas fire. That makes me feel a little better.

I thought we had some funny place names in Jamaica, like Maggoty and Middle Quarters, but Elephant and Castle beats just about everything. I've never lived in a big city before, never seen so much concrete or so many people and cars. None of the people look like me. I go from being surrounded by people who know me to being surrounded by strangers. I don't know what's happened to the sun. It still shines but it isn't hot. Also, the stars have gone and there are no frogs calling to each other at night.

"This is your home now," my mother tells me as we eat breakfast on my first morning. "You can call your stepfather dad if you like."

I do, although it sounds strange. I haven't had a dad before. He is a nice man, a chef, and he does his best to treat me the same as his real son, Trevor, born in England. I have to take him to kindergarten around the corner as my mother leaves early for work. She works for the civil service, and is head of the typing pool on account of her good spelling and speedy fingers.

After two or three weeks' holiday – 'acclimatising' my mother calls it – we buy my school uniform, pens and pencils, a rubber, a ruler and exercise books. The first day arrives. I haven't even made it through the school gates before I hear a shout.

"Oi! Where're you going, mate?"

I turn around to see a boy – bigger than me – leaning against a brick wall. He ambles over, with some friends in tow. I don't say anything. It's odd. He's smiling but doesn't look very friendly.

"School is for kids, not monkeys," he says, making monkey noises and putting his fists up. I drop my bag and raise my fists too. My dad has told me I might need to stand up for myself sooner rather than later. I take a swing but he ducks out of the way and my punch doesn't land. His friends jeer and a crowd gathers round, chanting "Fight! Fight!"

"Break it up, boys!" A teacher strides out through the gates, taking in the situation. "And leave him alone," he adds, talking to the bigger boy. Now that the show's over, everyone starts trooping into school.

"See you in the playground," the bigger boy mouths at me before going off with his friends. I spend the rest of the day with my eyes down and my mouth shut. I don't want any more trouble.

I trudge home after school, put the key in the door and am greeted by the empty flat. I hang up my coat, take off my shoes and drop my school bag in my room. I feel so alone. I don't understand anything about this new world. All I have ever known is Mountain Side.

Back in Jamaica, trouble was a bad dog that always barked at me from behind some rusty iron gates on my walk to school. One day, the gates were open. I picked up some small stones and crept past, hoping the dog was inside the house. I hadn't gone far when fierce barking behind me made a helter-skelter feeling in my tummy. I spun round and flung some of the stones at the dog running full pelt towards me. They missed, but the dog stopped in its tracks. It looked at me with a puzzled expression and wagged its tail. A game to it was war to me.

Perhaps it was just a game to the boy today too. Maybe he was just testing me.

On my way back from the kitchen with the sandwich Mum left in the fridge for me, I see Granny looking at me from the photograph on the mantelpiece. I flop down on the couch, imagine Granny's strong hands rubbing my back. Soon I'm munching the sandwich. Everything will work out all right, I think. I will find my way.

The first thing is to learn a Cockney accent. No one outside the family understands me and I'm finding it hard to make out what anyone is saying to me. Over the next few weeks, I try out the new sounds in shops where no one knows me. Soon I sound like the other boys.

One evening, when my mum passes me a plate of macaroni cheese, instead of saying "Tanks!" I say "Fanks!"

She, my dad and Trevor all stop what they're doing and look at me.

"You're becoming a Londoner!" Mum says and we all laugh.

And do you know what?

I'm beginning to feel like one.

FACT FILE

BRITAIN AFTER
THE WAR

Britain had a labour shortage after the Second World War and needed people to come and help rebuild the country. Although there were lots of jobs available, life in Britain after the war was still hard in many ways. Food was rationed and the Germans had bombed several cities, so many buildings and homes were in a bad state. Australia also wanted lots of people to come to their country after the war. They only wanted white people, in particular white British people. This was called the 'White Australia' policy. So, tempted by the idea of better weather and an easier life, thousands of white British men, women and children went to Australia after the war.

At least another 70,000 white British women left Britain to settle in the USA and Canada as 'war brides'. During the war many white servicemen from Canada and the USA were stationed in Britain. Sometimes they married white British women and started families with them. After the war, these servicemen returned to their countries and the new brides joined their husbands.

At the same time many people from the Caribbean were coming to Britain in the decades after the war. Britain's Caribbean colonies were poor and there were not many jobs or good opportunities for most people. The best jobs and opportunities were kept for white British and local white Caribbean people.

War brides of American serviceman arrive in New York with their children

Prime Minister Winston Churchill visits bombed out buildings in the East End of London on 8 September 1940

43

ELIZA KING IS AT HOME

KATY MASSEY

Ilive in Stepney, and Stepney is where everybody used to come first. Now people coming from Africa and the Caribbean settle all around London, especially in Brixton and Notting Hill. But last century, the East End was the place for new arrivals, as it is too close to the London Docks to be decent enough for proper Londoners to live in. I am not from here – I am not from anywhere really – but I love Stepney.

It is not pretty though. The tall, terraced buildings are dirty from pollution. Some used to have shops downstairs, but now most are boarded up, giving the place a closed-down look. People say Stepney is poor, which is true. And they say the streets are dangerous after dark, but they're not if you know where to avoid. In my life, I've found it's more dangerous for me to be among people who thought they were kind. Now, I prefer to be among my own people.

Stepney is so different from where I grew up. In Yorkshire, I didn't see one other person who looked like me. I came to London to find my people and was lucky enough to meet my husband. He is from Somalia, so we opened a boarding house for Somali seamen here. That was over twenty years ago. I'd never had a proper home before and I love providing somewhere comfortable for these men, and looking after them. After all, they are so far away from the place they were born. They need all kinds of advice, about how to keep warm, how to behave and where to find a job. I even wash and mend their clothes.

People of all colours and all religions have settled here: Stepney is even in the Domesday Book. I could show you the world in an afternoon; not only Africans and West Indians, but Arabian, Maltese and Asian people, too. It is wonderful! They call it 'London's Harlem' or 'The Coloured Quarter' in the newspapers. And, though there isn't an official border between where we live and where the white people live, we seem to agree not to go into each other's areas. A white person has never once invited me into their house.

So here at our boarding house, I teach newcomers the rules, but they are very complicated. For example, a man from the Caribbean or Africa can work for the Royal Mail if he has been in the British Forces, but if he hasn't, forget it! And he can work at Marylebone Station as a porter, but not at Euston Station. If he turns up there, they will tell him there are no jobs, no matter how short of bodies they are. In the future, I hope there are no limitations as to where a Black man can and can't work, and where he can and can't live. But for now, it's up to me and my husband to teach the new arrivals the rules and explain what is and isn't possible.

It is even more difficult now, as more and more men are coming to the house who were never seamen, but are instead stowaways. They have hidden on ships bound for Britain because they couldn't afford the fare. Bashiir was one such stowaway, but I must admit, I treated him more like a son than a boarder.

Bashiir was small and slight, like a long-distance runner. He had huge liquid brown eyes and thick black lashes. But what really set him apart were his beautiful manners. He learned how to behave working in a rich merchant's house just outside Mogadishu, Somalia's capital. After the Second World War, there was violence in Mogadishu and his master's home was destroyed. He told me he struggled on for a few years, before deciding to take his chances on board a ship bound for Europe. He eventually ended up at Tilbury Docks. Someone suggested he tried our boarding house, so he turned up on the doorstep with a nervous smile to ask if he might stay with us for a while.

One day, a few weeks after he arrived, he didn't come down for breakfast. By late afternoon, he still hadn't come down, so I went up to his room to find him. I stood in our narrow corridor and knocked on the door. There was no reply, so I gingerly turned the handle and entered. There he was, under the covers, curled up like a baby in the middle of his single bed. I could not miss him, because the room was so small, with only room for the bed, a small bedside table and a wardrobe.

Straight away I was worried. I had seen many lads cry tears of homesickness and dislocation, but I was surprised to see Bashiir like this. He was always the same: smiling, cheerful and so polite. Whatever could be the matter? I tried to be gentle.

"What is it my boy? Are you feeling ill?"

"No! I'm fine thank you, Eliza." His quiet voice came from beneath the thin blanket. It was immediately followed by a loud, damp sob he had no hope of hiding.

I perched on the corner of the mattress, which groaned under the weight of two people. "Come on, Bashiir. You can tell me. Has someone hurt you? Or stolen something from you? Whatever it is, it has happened before and I will know what to do. I promise."

There was a long pause.

"There is nothing to do, Hooyo. That's the problem. I can't even look for a job until my papers come through from the Colonial Office."

He'd called me Hooyo – Mother – and I felt warm inside, but he stayed underneath his blanket. I understood what it was like to feel useless and ashamed, and I wanted to help him.

"Why don't you go out for a walk? Get some fresh air?"

"Fresh! Ha! You can cut the smog with a knife. And anyway, where can I go? I don't have any money and even if I did, I don't like these people. They are rough. They have no manners!"

I could tell he thought that, after a dangerous journey hidden on a boat, he had finally arrived in England only for his hopes and dreams to lie in ruins. But he had so much further to go. I decided to tell him the same story I had told so many young men before him: my story.

"You came here hiding on a boat, and I was brought here from Ethiopia by missionaries. We both have to make the best of it, Bashiir."

"I didn't know that..."

"Oh yes! They took me from my home when I was very little. We travelled all the way to Yorkshire. This was before the first war. I don't know why they took me. Perhaps my parents had died? I never found out. At church meetings I had to stand on a table and be stared at, so they could show people what a 'heathen' was. Then the missionaries died and I was put in an orphanage. There, I wasn't allowed to mix with the other girls. I couldn't even read until I ran away and a kind man I worked for taught me how. So, you see Bashiir, I was rough and had no manners! I didn't even know that there was anybody else who had brown skin until I came to London."

"I can't believe that!" His small brown head had appeared from under the covers. "You are so kind to us, Hooyo. Putting warm bricks between my sheets to save me from the cold! How could they be so cruel?"

He was genuinely angry for me. Bashiir was sat up in bed now, his eyes wide. He had forgotten his troubles for a moment, at least.

"I came here to find my people," I told him. "Not just ones who looked like me, but who I could feel at home with, relax among. And you'll find yours Bashiir, I promise. It just might take a little time."

"OK, I am listening. And even if I can't feel your words now, because I am too sad, I know I will remember them in future…" He managed a small smile. "Can I help you make dinner? It will give me something to do."

"I have a few eggs, enough to make some malawah…"

I wasn't sure I had the right word for the Somali flatbreads, but I felt sure they would cheer him up.

"Oh Hooyo, thank you! I will help you stir the mixture, and we will talk and I will feel better."

Bashiir was like that. With a little encouragement he could find hope anywhere. But I knew he had no family left alive in Somalia, so perhaps it helps to have no choice.

And that set a pattern. After that day, we would cook dinner together and talk. We didn't only make African food, but whatever we could to stretch the rations. I told him all about the history of Stepney, how it was the place for seamen who worked on the merchant ships to spend their time on land, before they caught another ship home. Of course, some stayed, so there have been Black people here for hundreds of years. John Wilkes was the earliest we know about. He was baptized at St Dunstan's in 1780 but he probably wasn't the first, just the first written down in the Parish Register.

Not long after that first meal we cooked together, I was walking down Cable Street, looking around at all of the broken-down houses. Hitler's bombs came down hard on the dockside areas, to try and destroy the ships. Some of the streets were so badly bombed during the war; they looked like mouths full of broken teeth. Christmas was approaching and the weather had turned bitter and cruel. Plenty of people who couldn't afford to rent a proper room lived in bomb-damaged buildings, camping like squatters. I thought of how freezing some of them must be.

I turned into Leman Street and passed Colonial House, another hostel. This one had been set up by the government's Colonial Office. A dozen or so men who lived there hung around on the cracked stone steps up to the house's entrance. They looked cold, chatting in a bored way. Frost had begun settling on the weeds growing in the gaps between the paving stones, but the men had nothing to do and nowhere safe to go. No wonder the neighbours called it 'The Government Gambling House'.

So, I started to think of a way to get the Black community together. I have lived here almost my whole life, but it is a cold and sometimes unfriendly place. Gangs of young Britons would sometimes come around after dark, looking for trouble. Some of the men in the hostel were scared to go out into the world and try to make friends. I wanted to show Bashiir, and men like him, that it was possible to have fun here. I had the idea that it would be good for them to mix with families who had settled well and built a good life in England. The men who had started to feel hopeless would learn that it was possible to be happy here, even if their mothers and fathers were thousands of miles away. I believe you can find family anywhere, if your heart is open.

Then it hit me: a Christmas party! My husband and I had already started the Stepney Coloured People's Association to help our people. We held evening classes, and taught reading and writing to help the men get better jobs. We ran the association with Ghanaians, Indians, Yorubans and Somalians. Bashiir had started learning to read and write English at our classes – he could already speak it.

I wasn't sure how I was going to organize a party, but I believe there's always a way to get something done. First, I tried to find a hall to hold it in. I got turned down by so many people. "I can't vouch for your behaviour," said one woman, shaking her head before I'd finished speaking.

A man at the Methodist Church said, "You can have the hall if your members will come to church."

"We have Muslims, Hindus, Roman Catholics, agnostics, all sorts," I told him. "You can't expect them to give it up!"

Eventually I went to the council and they let us have the town hall for the day.

We had a glorious party. Lots of poor children and their families came, and the *Daily Mirror* sent us a huge hamper of food and presents to share out. Best of all, we had a beautiful Black Father Christmas. He was from Ghana and had a big belly. He was so jolly and cuddly, everyone loved him.

To see all our people together smiling, laughing and having a good time, well, I was in heaven. We gave each other the strength to face the New Year with pride. We had refreshed each other's souls and knew that we belonged somewhere at last. When I looked over at Bashiir, he had tears of joy in his eyes, and I knew he felt it, too.

Soon after Christmas, Bashiir's papers came through and he got a job working for the concierge at The Ritz, a hotel in the West End. It is a fine establishment and suited his good looks and beautiful manners perfectly. He moved out of the boarding house and into a small bed-sitting room in a different part of London.

That was quite a few years ago now, but I still remember him. I think of his good manners and his quiet strength and hope he's happy wherever he is. I hope he's found his people. And I hope he remembers me: his Hooyo.

FACT FILE

HUBERT 'BARON' BAKER

• •

Hubert 'Baron' Baker was born in Jamaica. During the Second World War he came to Britain as a Royal Air Force (RAF) policeman. After the war in Europe ended, Baron decided to stay in Britain.

When he heard that the *Empire Windrush* was coming with hundreds of ex-RAF servicemen on board, Baron wondered where those who had nowhere to stay would sleep and live. No one had a clue! So Baron suggested Clapham South deep-level shelter and his suggestion was accepted. Deep-level shelters are a network of tunnels built deep under London's underground stations. They were used during the war for people to shelter safely during bombing.

Baron went to greet the *Windrush*. He helped more than two hundred men have somewhere to sleep and food to eat while they found a job. The Clapham South deep-level shelter is very near to Brixton. There were already a few African-Caribbean and West African families living in Brixton. Many of the people who arrived on the *Empire Windrush* and stayed in the Clapham South deep-level shelter found jobs and settled in Brixton. And, to this day, Brixton is associated with African-Caribbean people and culture – all because of Baron Baker's idea.

Ten years later, in 1958, Baron helped the Black community again. He used his training as an RAF policeman to help the Black community protect themselves against attacks from racist gangs in Notting Hill.

Right: men temporarily living in the Clapham South deep-level air raid shelter, London, 22 June 1948

• •

DIARY OF A WINDRUSH KID

JERMAIN JACKMAN

23 December 1952

Dear Diary,

This is my first ever diary entry. My mum got me this diary as an early Christmas present, even though I would've preferred the skipping rope I asked for. Mum says all the greatest explorers have diaries to take on journeys with them, so I should have one too. I'm not sure why I need one though, as I'm not an explorer, and I don't have any journeys planned.

Well, I have no idea what else to write about, so let me introduce myself. I'm Georgina, but everyone calls me Baby G because I have a baby face. I'm nine years old and I live in a village just outside Georgetown, Guyana. I go to Plaisance Methodist School and I love swimming.

My mum is a nurse at Georgetown Public Hospital and my dad works as a miner in Guyana's gold mines. I only get to see him once every five months. Mum says that's because he works really hard and really far away.

My favourite place to go is the seawall that protects our village from high tides. My mum says we have the seawall because our country sits below sea level. It's always patrolled and maintained by the Colonial Government because Guyana is part of the British Colony.

I love my family, I love my friends, and did I already say I really love swimming?

24 December 1952

Dear Diary,

I hate my family and I hate my friends! I know what I said yesterday but ignore that. Now I know why Mum got me this diary. She just told me we're moving to England! ENGLAND! That's the journey she spoke about. We leave on New Year's Day – that is eight days away. I only have EIGHT DAYS LEFT!

When I told my friends about moving, they were happy and excited for me. I was so confused! Don't they like me? Why do they want me to go away? I don't want to go – I want to stay!

I had to ask Mum why we were going. She said, "I know it's upsetting Baby G but your dad and I believe this for the best, things aren't perfect here for us."

She reached out to show me the magazine in her hand and said, "Come, look at the list of nursing jobs I could get in the mother country, they pay more than I could ever imagine!"

She excitedly turned the page and continued "Baby G, look at the schools! That's a better education for you. How many times have I said, education is key to the life you want, you understand?"

But I like my life here, I like my school HERE! Mum went to school here and she turned out fine – why do I have to be different. It's just not fair.

25 December 1952

Dear Diary,

It's Christmas Day and I'm still upset but I'm feeling a bit better than yesterday. That's only because my dad is the one person who knows how to cheer me up. He came home late last night while I was sleeping then, early this morning, he woke me up to see the warm Christmas Day sun rise in the distance. He sat me on his lap and sang the same sweet song he sings to me every Christmas.

"I saw three ships come sailing in on Christmas Day, on Christmas Day. I saw three ships come sailing in on Christmas Day in the morning."

He looked at me and said, "We only had enough money for two people, so it will be your mum who goes with you to London. When she's made enough money, she'll send for me."

He smiled and told me all the stories he's heard about the mother country.

He said that the queen lives there, that there will be loads of children my age to play with and the roads are paved with gold, milk and honey. Sounds yummy to me!

26 December 1952

Dear Diary,

I woke up this morning with an upset stomach. I think I ate too much yesterday but Christmas Day was perfect. Mum made pepperpot, our country's national dish, and there's still some left over.

I'll be honest; I'm sort of changing my mind about our journey to England. Thinking about what Dad said, a part of me (a small part) is slowly getting excited and wants to go. But the other part of me is still sad and wants to stay.

I don't have long left to say my goodbyes, so today my friends and I decided to go swimming. We spent all afternoon by the shoreline, splashing in the sea, laughing and having fun until it got dark and then Mum came to fetch me.

When I got home, I found all these huge suitcases that my mum had bought from the market. "Baby G, you always leave things to the last minute. Could you start packing now please?" Mum said, passing me one of the bags. "I'll come and help you in a bit."

So, it looks like no more beach trips for me. I'm going to spend the next few days packing.

31 December 1952

Dear Diary,

Today was my final day at school. It was really sad to say goodbye to all the friends I've grown up with. I don't know how I'm going to make new friends in England. What if nobody likes me?

I think Mum knew I was upset when I came home from school because she made her famous tuna sandwiches and cut them into triangles, without the crust, just how I like them. Dad took the day off work so we could spend the last evening together. We had dinner and he helped me and Mum to finally finish packing everything. We piled the suitcases up by the front door, so we're ready to leave tomorrow morning.

Well, there's not much I can do now other than cry myself to sleep, I'm really going to miss home.

1 January 1953

Dear Diary,

Dad woke me up early this morning with a whisper, "Happy New Year".

We watch the sun rise over the village for the last time together. The air was nice and cool, the breeze was gentle and silent, but the neighbour's rooster ruined the peace with its morning crows. I hate that rooster!

I got dressed and started to feel really nervous. I had never been to an airport, let alone on a plane before. I didn't know what to expect. Mum told me the journey would be very long. She said something about taking the plane to Trinidad and then a ship from there to Barcelona in Spain. After that we'll take the train to Calais and another boat to Dover and finally trainbound to London, where the Queen lives!

I don't think I'll be able to write during the journey, as I need to pack away my diary now, but I will when I get to London. Pray for me!

18 January 1953

Dear Diary,

Oh my gosh! So much has happened over the last few weeks, I don't even know where to start! Firstly, that journey was so long and I found out I suffer from seasickness the hard way. The propeller planes were so shaky and the boat was so rocky, especially when it was stormy. I couldn't sleep at all. I remembered Dad telling me this story about a small boat he was in that turned over on his way to the gold mines, and I was fearful it might happen to us. So, most nights Mum and me just prayed.

Secondly, ENGLAND IS VERY COLD! We arrived in the middle of the afternoon and it was freezing! Mum saw me shivering and gave me a long-sleeved cardigan from her bag, but it didn't help much.

Thirdly, there is no sunshine. It is dull here and kind of miserable. Back in Guyana, the birds are vibrant and brightly coloured but here the birds are grey.

Fourthly, people here aren't very kind. I nearly got separated from my mum when we got to the big train station in London because people were pushing us out of their way. I'm used to saying, "good morning", "good afternoon" and "good night" to people in my village. But here nobody gives a friendly greeting. There are so many people and everyone is always in a rush.

I really miss home. I miss my friends. All I think about is the warmth, food and fun back in Guyana. I don't like it here. Mum says I haven't even given England a chance and that I should wait to see how my first day at school goes.

On a good note, there's a friendly old lady who lives down the hall and she baked a cake for us. My mum didn't let me eat it though. I think it's because she saw the lady wipe her nose with her hand before she gave it to us.

Tomorrow is a big day for me. It's my first day at school. I'm feeling really nervous but excited to make new friends. Wish me luck!

19 January 1953

Dear Diary,

I had high hopes for my first day of school, but it turned out to be terrible. People said Baby G was a silly name, and I was called names. I didn't even know the meaning of. I felt so alone and isolated.

Mum works really long hours as an NHS nurse at the hospital but she was able to come to collect me from school and I told her what happened. She decided to take me out for a meal, even though I knew it was expensive to eat out here. There were a few places to eat on the same street as my new school, but Mum kept on walking past them and told me to ignore the signs. She was walking so fast I didn't get a chance to even read them.

We finally found a nice place to eat and sat down inside. I was so hungry and was really looking forward to having some fish and chips, but no one came to our table. Then Mum got up to place our order and for some reason the man behind the counter started shouting at her. I got really scared. He said, "No Blacks allowed", and pointed at a sign in the window. I've seen these signs before. I can't understand why some people have decided they don't like us. They haven't even met us.

29 June 1953

Dear Diary,

I've been going to school for a few months now and things have got a bit better. My teacher, Miss Williams, is nice to me. She said she likes my accent even though everyone else says I talk funny. Miss Williams let me write on the blackboard and told me I have very nice handwriting.

Oh, and I have made a friend! Her name is Rebecca. She's really nice; she's tall and has thick black hair like me, and her birthday is two days before mine. She hates being called Becky or Becca because she thinks it sounds too English, which is funny because she was born here.

She told me her dad was a Jamaican soldier who stayed here after the war and her mum is English, that's why Rebecca's skin is a bit lighter than mine. The other children treat her like they treat me. They call us coloured. She tells me that racism is really bad but not everyone in England is like that.

5 July 1953

Dear Diary,

Yesterday Rebecca and I went swimming. I was so excited as I've wanted to go swimming since we left Guyana. I asked Rebecca where the seaside was because I loved swimming in Guyana and she laughed and said the closest thing we have to a seaside is the River Thames, and trust me you don't want to swim in that.

We went inside this big building and it smelled funny but Rebecca quickly changed into her swimming costume and jumped in the water and I followed behind her.

I had so much fun! I had loads of space to swim because when we jumped in a lot of people left the pool. Rebecca told me that some people don't like swimming with Black people, but she just ignored it when people moved away from us, so I did too.

When we got out, my eyes were burning. Rebecca said something about a chemical called chlorine that they put in the water and that I should just wash my face in the showers.

18 July 1953

Dear Diary,

I'm really worried about Mum. She came home crying. I didn't know if it was something I'd done or if something had happened at work but I had never seen her cry before. When she went to the shared kitchen to make us dinner, I heard her talking to the old lady from down the hall.

She said, "I heard so many good things about England, the land of opportunity where the streets were paved with gold. But I'm finding it hard, Baby G is finding it hard."

"What do you mean?" the old lady down the hall replied.

"As a mother, I have a duty to protect and provide for my daughter and I was struggling to do that in Guyana. I just feel like I'm struggling here too. The racist abuse from random people is relentless, on top of being made to feel like we don't belong.

"But I'm reminded of Baby G and her future, so I try to protect her from all of that. They have universities here; the schools, the books and the equipment are all better here. The thought of her success in this mother country makes everything worthwhile," she whispers through her tears.

I finally understood. Mum moved here for me. Everything she has ever done was for me. To give me a better start in life. And all I've ever done is complain. Mum works so hard to protect me and gives me everything to make sure I succeed.

I don't want to just tell her how much I appreciate everything she does – I want to show her. So, dear diary, I'm turning a new page today. Starting fresh. And aiming high, no matter what!

68 years later...

30 September 2021

Dear Diary,

It has been nearly seventy years since I last picked up this diary. I thought I lost it when we moved house. And I happened to find it, by chance. My granddaughter is asking me for pictures of when I first arrived here for her Windrush project at school. These diary entries have brought back a lot of memories.

So much has happened to the folks that arrived with me to these shores many years ago. A few years after arriving in London, my mum saved up enough to bring my dad over, who later worked on the train lines during the night. Both my parents returned to Guyana to live out the rest of their retirements together while I stayed here to build a family with the man of my dreams. We've been married for forty years with three wonderful children and seven amazing grandchildren.

When I look back at my life and our journey to England, I am filled with such admiration for the huge bravery it took, to leave behind everything my mum knew in Guyana, in search for a better life for me. Well, I am proud to say, it was worth it. Although tough and at times, near impossible, I was top of all my classes, studied health and social care in college and midwifery at university to follow in my mother's footsteps and work in the NHS.

But my days of delivering babies are over. However, I am forever grateful and proud for the contributions made by my parents and so many others who took the decision to make the journey from the West Indies to here, our mother country.

This will be my final diary entry, but not the end of my journey, because it will live on through the journey my granddaughter is about to make.

Much love,
A Windrush Kid x

FACT FILE

THE NATIONAL
HEALTH SERVICE

• •

Before the NHS people had to pay for their healthcare. It was expensive and even middle class people often struggled to find the money to pay for a visit to the doctor.

Britain's NHS was officially launched on 5 July 1948. In the late 1950s and in the 1960s Britain needed more nurses to come to work for the NHS. So they asked people to come from other countries in the Caribbean, parts of Africa and Asia and from Ireland. Soon many of Britain's nurses were Black women from the Caribbean and Africa. Without the Black nurses the NHS wouldn't have survived.

A Jamaican nurse, circa 1960

SAM KING

Sam King came to Britain from Jamaica during the Second World War. He served in the Royal Air Force. Later on Sam went back to Jamaica but decided to return to Britain on the *Empire Windrush* in June 1948. Sam became the first Black mayor of Southwark. He said, "The future will be good if we go about it carefully. We from the ex-colonies have contributed a lot to the improvement of the British way of life. In 1948 nearly a third of the inner cities were destroyed by bombing – we helped to rebuild it."

Former *Windrush* passenger and member of the RAF Sam King MBE

A NIGHT IN LONDON

1948 – ST CATHERINE, JAMAICA

KIRSTY LATOYA

Tyson stood unnervingly still, staring at Shanika with a mischievous look. She glanced past him, searching for an escape route. She was so close to home but had to outsmart her biggest fear first. The Jamaican sun was hot and sweat dripped down her neck. She quickly stepped to the left and Tyson copied; she stepped right and he mirrored her again. A few leaflets by Shanika's foot caught her eye. They were recruitment posters from the British Government. Having little importance to the eight-year-old, she decided to scrunch them up and throw them at her enemy. As she slowly bent down, Tyson darted towards her. Startled, Shanika fell backwards; as she scrambled to her feet, Tyson pounced on her. Her four-legged foe, no bigger than her school bag, stood on her chest and licked her face uncontrollably. Shanika hated dogs, but this puppy had taken a liking to her.

The puppy's owner laughed from a nearby veranda and shouted "You still 'fraid of the dawg?" Tyson ran back to his owner, wagging his tail.

Shanika stood up, brushed down her khaki school uniform and set off for home. At least this was the last time she'd have to see that puppy.

Tucking into her oxtail dinner that evening, Shanika entertained her mother with stories of her near-death experience at the paws of Tyson.

Her mother, Marie, laughed. "One day you have to get over that fear, yuh nuh! Whole heap of dogs deya England!"

Marie and Shanika started giggling together. Shanika loved her mum and how much fun they had, but she missed her dad dearly. Shanika had been her father's sidekick when he'd lived in Jamaica. He'd taken her everywhere with him. She'd loved riding in the front seat of his bright red Ford truck. It made her feel like the most important person in the world. That feeling seemed so distant now though. It had been a whole year since she had seen him, but there was only one more sleep until that was about to change.

The tall palm trees, bright blue skies and clear blue waters of her home transformed into tall brown buildings, depressing grey clouds and busy, bustling streets. Shanika stared out of the car window at her new surroundings, taking it all in. This was worlds away from her sunny St Catherine home. Excitement had quickly turned into exhaustion; the plane, bus and train rides had been an ordeal for the pair.

Marie sat in the front seat, hugging herself to keep warm. Her flimsy cotton jacket was no match for the London weather. The driver, a workmate of Marie's husband, had volunteered to pick them up from the train station and drop them off at Gerald's accommodation. They pulled up into a quiet residential street where cars lined either side of the narrow road. The mother and child were about to be reunited with the most important person in their lives and they couldn't stop smiling.

Knock, knock, knock.

They waited patiently outside the house and soon a light flicked on inside. A tall, middle-aged woman with fair skin and bright blue eyes opened the door. Assessing the pair in front of her, she folded her arms and asked rudely, "And who may you be?"

"Good evening, miss," Marie replied. If she was stunned at the woman's tone, she didn't show it. "I got this address from mi husband Gerald, this is his daughter. Is he home?" The woman took note of the heavy accent and the suitcases.

"Did you just come from Jamaica or something? We don't get a lot of coloured people round here."

Embarrassed, Marie clutched the handle of her suitcase tighter.

"Gerald did not tell me you were coming," the woman continued, without waiting for an answer. "He's not home and you can't come in!"

The woman shut the door abruptly, making Shanika jump. A feeling of dread washed over Marie. They were alone in a country she had never been to before and she didn't know what to do.

The bitter November night was unkind to the pair; shivering they walked down the street, looking for somewhere warm to rest and wait for Gerald. The dream of moving to a better place and saving the 'mother country' was slowly wearing off. It was becoming a nightmare. Shanika pointed out a bus stop in view of the house and they made their way over to it. The extra layers from their suitcases didn't help with the harsh cold and their fingers became numb. Where was Gerald?

Shanika marvelled at the phenomenon of seeing her breath in front of her; she had never been so cold. Two more hours passed and they saw nobody enter or leave the house. There were no buses and hardly any cars.

"Right," Marie said standing up. "We can't stay here all night, let's find somewhere to stay." It was eleven o'clock by the time the pair started trailing the streets of North London. Tomorrow they would go back to Gerald's place and work it out.

They soon found a house with a 'Rooms available' sign in the window. Marie knocked lightly and a woman in a dressing gown appeared in the doorway.

"Do you know what time it is?" the woman barked, her hands on her hips.

"Good evening ma'am, mi sorry to knock—" Marie replied, as Shanika shrunk back.

"Did you not see the other sign?" the woman interrupted, pointing to another window. In faded letters, Marie could just about make out the words 'No coloured people'. The woman shut the door and Marie and Shanika stood open-mouthed on the doorstep.

Eight houses and eight failed attempts later, Shanika was struggling to keep up with her mum as she marched down the street. They were still no closer to securing a warm bed for the night. The last landlord had poked his head around the curtain to see who was at the door, then pretended not to be home when he realized it was Black people.

Marie had never come across such unpleasant and unwelcoming people. They had been walking for hours; she didn't know where her husband was, her daughter was cold and she was losing hope.

"Mum, I can't feel my fingers or my toes."

"I know baby, me neither." She couldn't fight the tears any longer, they streamed down her cheeks. As they approached yet another house, Shanika suggested they pray, like they did back home on Sundays. Before they could finish their prayer, a ginger-haired man opened the front door.

"God heard you! I saw you from my window," the man said with a thick Irish accent. "It'll cost ya 40 shillings for the night."

Marie thanked him and the pair followed him into his poorly lit house and walked up a few flights of stairs. Marie threw the suitcases down and got into bed with her daughter. It wasn't very warm but it sure was better than the streets.

The next morning, before Marie had even opened her eyes, the landlord rushed in.

"Time to get going, I don't want to upset the rest of my tenants."

Shanika asked why they'd be upset and he explained he only took British people in. England sure seemed to have a lot of rules about which people were allowed to do what!

Back on the streets, there was nowhere to go but back to Gerald's house. The same woman opened the door. "Oh, it's you again," she said. "Gerald didn't come home last night. I don't think he's coming back."

Shanika thought something about her tone seemed off, but Marie thanked her politely and walked away. What were they going to do now?

With hungry bellies, Marie and Shanika went in search of something to eat. Whilst searching they passed a sign in a house window 'No blacks, No dogs, No Irish'. It was clear this place was a lot different to Jamaica.

Shanika spotted a corner shop and they walked towards it. After picking up snacks they stood in the queue, waiting to pay,

"Mum," Shanika whispered. "Why are they serving everyone before us?"

The shopkeeper must have overheard, as he ushered them over to pay, probably hoping they wouldn't cause a fuss.

"Mum, I don't like this place," Shanika said as they left the shop. "What if we never find Dad?"

"We will, Shani," replied Marie, but she was starting to worry about the same thing.

They walked to a park across the road and sat on a bench to eat their sandwiches and snacks, using their suitcases as tables. Marie flicked through her address book, looking for phone numbers of people in England that she could call. After they'd finished eating, she headed to the phone box at the entrance of the park, leaving Shanika with instructions to watch the bags and not talk to anyone.

As the phone rang, Marie watched her daughter in the distance, feeding the pigeons her crusts. Nobody answered on the first number she tried, so Marie dialled another, then looked over to check on Shanika. There was somebody standing in front of her. The tall figure had a coat and hat on and appeared to be talking to her. Marie shot out of the phone box, leaving the phone dangling. She ran towards her child, preparing to save her from this stranger danger. As she approached the bench, the figure turned around and Marie stopped dead in her tracks.

"Is that any way to greet yuh husband?" the man said. Tears filled her eyes.

"GERALD!" Their embrace was sweeter than the pair had imagined. When they finally let go of each other, Marie noticed an extra suitcase.

"Mi landlady told me this morning that you came. I was home the whole time. She lied to you, mi sorry baby." He paused to kiss his wife on the forehead. "She told me you couldn't stay in mi room, even if mi pay more, so I told her mi leaving. I was asking all around town for you guys."

"I can't believe you found us, it's been so bad." Marie rested her head on his chest and their daughter joined their embrace. In this strange, cold country, their love warmed their souls.

"I spoke to mi auntie in Brixton, she said we can go and stay with her. There's more Black people there too," Gerald reassured his family. "I'll have to travel to the garage for work but it's not too long."

"I just want to be with you and Shani. Mi love yuh both." Shanika looked up at her parents; this moment was so special to her. No matter how cold it was or how mean people had been, all that mattered was the love they shared. That love would get them through anything.

Just at that moment, a dog ran through their legs, interrupting their precious moment. Shanika screamed and jumped on to the bench. The dog barked up at her.

"Shani, you still 'fraid of dawg?" Gerald asked, trying not to laugh.

"Yes!" said Shanika and Marie in unison.

The dog leaped on to the bench and began licking Shanika's ankles. She shrieked again.

"It's OK, baby! It's just being friendly," said Marie.

Shanika took a deep breath and tried to be brave. The dog wasn't trying to eat her; it was trying to be nice. She bent down and gave it a cautious pat. The dog licked her hand excitedly. If she could move to a new country and start a new life, she could get over her fear of dogs, too.

"Shani, you remember mi red truck?" Gerald asked.

Shanika nodded excitedly. "Do you have one here?"

"Not yet," her father replied. "But I've got something else red I want to show you."

The family trekked through the park with their luggage. They turned on to a main road, and waited at a bus stop. A big red bus pulled up and Shanika's eyes lit up. Gerald paid the fare for them all and they hopped on. Marie and Shanika were in awe of the space inside the bus; it was much bigger than the ones in Jamaica. The family sat on the top deck laughing and joking, en route to a better future, together.

The *Empire Windrush* arriving at Tilbury Docks, 21 June 1948

Right: children arrived in Southampton, UK from the West Indies on the RMS *Ascania*, 3 June 1962

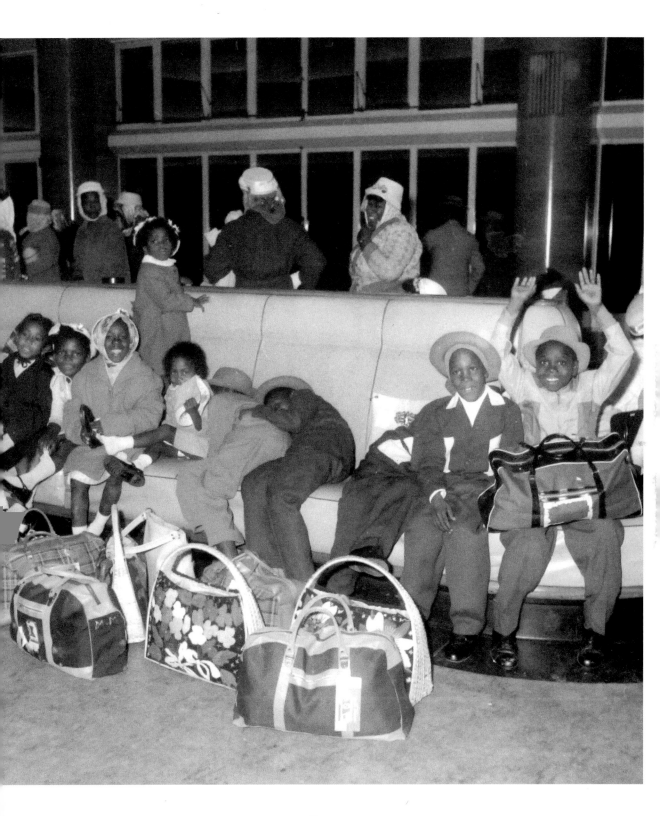

THE LIGHT AT THE END OF THE TUNNEL

KEVIN GEORGE

My name is Louvine, I grew up in Albert Town, Jamaica. Life in Albert Town was hard but good. When I wasn't spending time with my family, I would always be with my two best friends, Gloria and Gwendolyn. The three of us had gone to the same primary and secondary schools. After we'd finished school, we started doing odd jobs together, mostly for our families and friends. We were all still trying to figure out what type of work we really wanted to do. It was hard to earn a living in Albert Town, but we were young and having fun in the sun, so we tried not to worry too much.

It was 1948, a year that would be remembered for a few reasons. It started with the exciting news that Jamaica would be competing in the Olympics for the first time in the summer. As the weeks went by, however, the excitement began to get dampened by some strange rumours. The rumours changed depending on who you talked to, but they usually included the same four words: Jamaica, England, war and work.

Sometimes, one of our parents would send us to Albert Town Market to buy or sell something. The market was loud, busy and full of life. Everyone knew everyone. It was the place where rumours peaked. Everyone would carry their rumours to the market, mix them together and come up with the most colourful stories.

"Ya 'ear bout Hingland wanting to war wit Jamaica because the relationship nah work?" someone might say. Each story was as bad as the next. After a week or so, the stories became a running joke between me, Gloria and Gwendolyn.

No one took them too seriously, until a new pattern emerged. The stories swiftly changed from unlikely rumours to hushed questions: *Did you see the white men? Why are they here?* People were anxious because we didn't have many white people in Jamaica, and these white men were not there for a holiday. They wore suits and looked serious. We wondered what they wanted.

Like always, the market was a hotbed for conversation, but this time all the stories were similar, and, like dominoes, they were collapsing one by one in the same direction. The English wanted Jamaicans to help rebuild their country after the Second World War. Puzzle solved!

I felt relieved once I knew why the English men were there. I must give it to them, they left no stone unturned. They were everywhere, asking people to come and help England, and describing all the opportunities moving there would provide. It became a common sight to see an English man talking with a small huddle of Albert Town locals, and my curiosity would always guide me into the huddles. They made it sound great! Telling us that there were loads of jobs, that the wages were good, and although the country was not as warm as Jamaica, the people are. Unintentionally, I began to compare England to Albert Town, with England representing opportunity and Albert Town representing lack of opportunity.

One morning, when I was walking to the market with the girls, my head was filled up with thoughts of moving. I was torn between staying and going.

"Suttum nah right here," vocalizing the uncomfortable tussle between, staying in Albert Town or going to England.

"Yuh nah right, ow many times we seh stop tark to Johnny? Him nuh gud!" Gwendolyn chimed in. She never missed a chance to take the mickey. "Like yuh mudda seh, keep yuh ead inna book and off di boys."

I always found it hard to talk about my feelings, so when Gwendolyn jumped in with one of her jokes, I felt like I'd made the effort for no reason. Gloria, always the peacemaker of the group, chuckled but then said, "Him cheeky but him all right. Don't listen to Gwendolyn, ya hear?"

I kissed my teeth and asked them both, "What yuh tink about Hingland?"

"What yuh mean?" said Gwendolyn, responding in Gwendolyn fashion. "I tink Hingland is col', and di food nuh good."

"The hoppatunity, what yuh tink?" I responded. "Yuh wanna go?"

"No," Gwendolyn was sharp in her response.

"I do tink about it," Gloria said.

The conversation moved on. Us girls didn't really do serious conversations. Talking about leaving each other, our family, our home and everything we knew … it was too much to think about. Whenever times got tough, we would make jokes, ignore our feelings and keep moving forward. I could tell that the girls had already forgotten our conversation about England, but I hadn't.

A couple of days before I set off for England, Gloria and Gwendolyn came round and we headed to the market together one last time. Our parents didn't send us, and we had nothing to buy. This was our farewell walk and we shed some tears. I could tell Gwendolyn felt uncomfortable as she kept making jokes. Usually, her teasing annoyed me, but this time I didn't mind. I was feeling overwhelmed by everything and needed a break from all the emotions. Gloria and Gwendolyn's chatter was just what I needed to take my mind off things.

The day I left Jamaica, my mum, aunties and uncles came to the port to see me off. After I said my goodbyes to everyone and began walking towards the boat, I saw plenty of familiar faces from Albert Town and loads of the locals from the market. I started to feel more relaxed. The boat was huge! On the front in big, bold letters were the words *Empire Windrush*.

As I made my way on to the boat I began to worry about the lack of space. As big as the boat was, there were people everywhere and the conditions were not nice. We were crammed into tiny rooms, like animals in cages, and it was four to a bunk bed. It seemed the English wanted to squeeze as many of us as possible on that boat. I wasn't happy about it, but maybe it was part of the sacrifice for a better life.

When I arrived in England, I soon discovered that everything I'd been told had been oversold. I had to adjust to the reality of the England that I met, as well as the cultural differences. The food wasn't as fresh, the weather was cold and the people were always stressed. I wasn't sure if this was the kind of life I wanted, but I tried to stay positive. I knew that, for now, I needed to focus on settling in. But even that proved to be a challenge – a challenge because we were under attack! It wasn't England that was under attack – the war was long over – but us Black people certainly were. The Jamaicans who had come over to rebuild England after the war were being attacked by the very people they came to help – the English!

People would ignore us, put signs up to let us know we were not welcome, call us names and beat us up at night. There were even groups, drawn together by their hatred for us, that would roam the streets looking for trouble. One of these groups was known as the Teddy Boys. Most of the Teddy Boys had a similar look: big boots, tight trousers and hair drenched in Brylcreem. The area of West London I lived in, Notting Hill, was rife with Teddy Boys. They would terrorize the whole neighbourhood. If you were Black, you were advised not to be outside when it was dark. This made my life uncomfortable, as I found myself looking over my shoulder when leaving my home to do casual activities like food shopping, looking for jobs and going for walks so that I could get to know the area. It was tough, but I guess it was part of the sacrifice for a better life.

I spent most of my days, during my first month in England, looking for a job. The job search didn't feel as easy as the white men explained to us during our huddles in Albert Town. I would enquire about jobs after seeing the advertisement, only to be told that there was no job available. At first, I would look at the sign again, confused, wondering if I misread what was on there. Then I learned that there was a pool of jobs that Black people were more likely to be successful in achieving. They were what we referred to as 'helper jobs'. Jobs supplied by the government or large corporations that helped people and helped the country function, jobs in transport, nursing, cleaning and cooking. I focused on applying for cooking and nursing jobs, and within a couple of days I received my first job, as a nurse. I was so happy!

I enjoyed the job, and I made some good friends too, I formed a special bond with my fellow nurses, Hazel and Locus. Like me, they were from Jamaica. We would go shopping together and talk about anything and everything, with laughter being the theme of our trips. Being with Hazel and Locus, reminded me about the good old days with Gloria and Gwendolyn. I missed them and I missed Jamaica.

There were times when I looked back on everything I gave up for England and everything I put up with in England, and wondered if I made the right decision? The goal was always for a better life, but I didn't know what a better life was, so how would I have known what I was giving everything up for and whether it would have been worth it? With each sacrifice I saw the light at the end of the tunnel and I always saw this as a positive but after months of seeing the light, I began to think otherwise. Maybe leaving Jamaica was me leaving the light to get into the tunnel.

I would often hold these thoughts during times of frustration. However, as the years went by, I had those thoughts less and I began to feel more settled in England. I retired happy. Professionally, I progressed from Nurse to Chief Nursing Officer. Personally, I had three children and four grandchildren. I still meet up with Hazel and Locus, who are retired too, and we laugh with the same energy as we did on our shopping trips.

Reflecting on the sacrifices, the challenges and the friendships in my life, I learned that they all played a role in supporting me to shine brighter and help me to see that I am the light.

FACT FILE

A CALYPSONIAN
CALLED LORD WOODBINE

• •

Harold Adolphus Phillips was born in Trinidad and came to Britain during the Second World War to join the Royal Air Force. After the war he went back to Trinidad and performed his calypso songs on the streets.

In June 1948 he was one of the ex-RAF servicemen on board the *Empire Windrush*. Harold was the youngest of the three famous Trinidadian calypsonians on board the ship. They were called Lord Woodbine (Harold's stage name), Lord Kitchener (real name Aldwyn Roberts) and Lord Beginner (real name Egbert Moore). At first Harold lived in the Clapham South deep-level shelter until he found a job in Shropshire. Later, on Harold settled in Toxeth, Liverpool.

Harold toured England singing calypso and promoting steel pan music. He also became an early mentor, promoter and manager of a white British group called The Beatles who later became world famous.

'London is the Place for Me'
Aldwyn Roberts, under his calypso stage name Lord Kitchener, sang the now-famous 'London is the Place for Me' for reporters when the *Empire Windrush* arrived at Tilbury Docks in 1948. He was recorded by newsreel cameras. The song reflected the hopes and dreams of many passengers on board the ship.

• •

The Beatles in the Netherlands, 16 August 1960. Left to right: Beatles manager Allan Williams, his wife Beryl, Williams' business partner and calypso singer Lord Woodbine, Stuart Sutcliffe, Paul McCartney, George Harrison and Pete Best.

HALE AND HEARTY

SALENA GODDEN

The heat is high and dry, and the pot-holed track is hot and cracked beneath our best shoes. Arm in arm they go ahead: Charlie, Leila, Ben, Thelma, Michael and Sammy, walking home from choir practice. I am the smallest of seven and I walk slowly behind my six older siblings.

Mount Carmel Church has pale primrose yellow walls, so pretty against the bright and blue sky. We walk down the hill into the village square where the chickens peck at the ground near the feet of the lonely donkey tied to the post by the old well. Ahead and beyond I can look up and see the majestic Bull Head Mountain. I can almost feel the mountain vibrate with life, how she breathes in and out with all that lush jungle and emerald green. Bull Head Mountain is the soul of Clarendon – our village is called Colonels Ridge, it is our home.

Charlie, the tallest of all seven of us, starts to laugh as he says in a funny English accent, "I'm going go and take myself off to London!" He pushes his chin high, holds his pinkie up, his eyes wide, and pretends to twiddle an imaginary curly moustache. "I'll go and visit the Queen and we will have tea, oh la-di-da!"

How we all laugh together, all seven of us, all the way home down our lane. We walk and talk like really funny fancy London folk, all the way down the dusty lane towards home, passing the chickens in the village square and the lonely donkey tied to the post by the old well. I do not know then that this will be the last time we are all together, all seven of us, that this is the day everything will change.

When we get home, we begin our chores. My four brothers Charlie, Ben, Sammy and Michael chop and stack the wood. Michael is grumbling as usual, he is the laziest, always wanting to slope off and read books. Leila, the eldest, gives us jobs. There is always mending and cooking to do. Leila gives Thelma and I a basket of sewing and darning to do. Thelma is great with needlework, she wants to leave Colonels Ridge to be a dressmaker in Kingston one day, she makes all my dresses.

Leila sighs as she starts filling the sink with soapy water.

"What are you sighing at child?" Grandmother asks.

"Nothing, Mama…" Leila says, but she sighs again deeply, and you can tell it is not nothing at all. You can tell there is something big happening, but everyone is preoccupied and silent about it. Grandmother is sifting flour and I can tell she is thinking something big too. Our brothers chop the wood just outside the window by the side of the house, I can hear the small axe crack and split the logs as I sit and sew. I can tell the boys are brooding too, they don't make rude jokes and snigger about things, they work silently. Then when I look up from my sewing, I watch my sisters whispering and then Thelma is quietly asked to press Charlie's best Sunday shirt, which is strange as he only needs it for special occasions.

I want to ask everyone about the men that came into the chapel this afternoon. Those strange men that came with their shiny leather shoes and their big words and curly moustaches. The way they stood in their pressed and starched suits and fancy uniforms. They gave out pamphlets and said, "Your mother country needs you."

I think about the strangers, how they spoke with such authority and how they had interrupted our Christmas choir practice. We were in the middle of our rehearsal for next month, but they barged right in and said, "Do you mind if we talk to your music class?" Miss Rose said no, she did not mind. But you could tell Miss Rose did mind, she is very particular about the chapel choir rehearsals for the Christmas village concert, and she would not like us being called a *music class*. She bit her bottom lip, shook her fan open in front of her face and sat down. She began fanning herself rapidly as the men positioned themselves at the front to speak to us all. The men said they were speaking on behalf of the Queen of England. They spoke of many faraway places: Kingston, Dover, London, France and Germany; as they spoke, I recalled the map on the wall from school and tried to remember where these places were. They described long journeys in ships, they talked about honour and duty.

I look up from my needlework to watch Grandmother and her nimble fingers, how she makes quick work of kneading dough for dumplings. Her hands are all white with flour. She has wiped her hot brow and has flour marking her forehead. The kitchen smells so good, a delicious, sweet smell of home-roasted chicken, all spice and ginger.

Then suddenly the chickens out front begin to make a fuss, our two dogs, Dusty and Boo, begin to bark. There's the sound of a car engine and a commotion outside. Leila runs to the front porch. She roughly she wipes her hands on her apron as she goes. Men in suits and uniforms get out of their shiny silver car. It is more of the same foreign men from the chapel earlier. I notice how they sweat, how red their faces get in their suits in the heat.

"What's going on out there? What's all that racket?" Grandmother yells.

"It's the British officers again Mama..." Leila replies. "They are here to recruit eligible servicemen." She stands staring at them and wringing her hands on her apron and says under the breath, "I have never been to Kingston before."

Someone beeps the car horn. All the dogs along the lane are barking now. The rooster flaps and screeches too. There is so much fuss and noise. The sound of the men laughing. The men are all slapping each other's backs and shaking hands and grunting in agreement. I hear them repeating each other like this: "Because, you see, England is our mother country, and obviously if your mother has problems, you've got to go and help your mother!"

The British officers are parked in the road, right in front of my own porch. I know I am only eight years old but even I know they have come for one thing and that is to take my brothers and sisters away to war. They echo their talk from the chapel earlier "Your mother country needs you. We need fresh blood. We need strong and brave young people like you to join us and fight." Then one of the British officers passes out pamphlets to the gathering crowd. A leaflet falls and I run to pick it up and dash back to the safety of the porch. The leaflet says 'Your Mother Country Needs You' and lots of these big and clever words like *bravery*, *sacrifice*, *allegiance* and *obligation*.

My neighbour Tom, his brother Frank and his father have joined the crowd too. I watch from our porch as Tom's father writes his name on some papers. He shakes hands with the men in the suits and uniforms. Big John from church is next, he reaches for the pen. More and more villagers come and gather around the shiny silver car with the men with shiny-buttoned uniforms.

Then Grandmother comes out and stands on the porch to see what all the fuss is about. She kisses her teeth. She claps and dusts the flour from her hands. I see specks of the white flour in the dirt and our rooster comes over to peck at the nothing. Just then, as I look up, Charlie walks towards the English officers, then Ben and Sammy and Michael follow him. Thelma and Leila drift over and join the crowd too. As Charlie goes to shake an officer's hand, he throws down the small axe.

Time passes and with my brothers and sisters all gone away to help the war I am left all alone up on Colonels Ridge. It is just me and Grandmother and the two dogs, Dusty and Boo, and the greedy chickens and the noisy rooster and the lonely donkey tied to the post by the old well. It is quiet and lonesome on the edge of the Bull Head Mountain. Seems like everyone has gone on an adventure, gone away to sail on boats, to explore the big wide world and to fight wars for the Queen. All I do is stay home and go to school. I darn the socks and help Grandmother make dumplings. I go down to the river and listen to the mountain breathe on my own.

   When Christmas does finally come, there are only a few of us to sing in the choir for the Christmas concert, but we have to make up for our loud big brothers and sisters, so we sing as bold and bright and as jolly as we can, and we do a good show, and everyone claps, and it is as if we are doing our bit for the war too.

At Christmas time we have a letter from Leila...

Dear Mama,

How are you? How is everyone? I hope Dotty is still keeping up with her school and reading her books. Tell her to eat her greens and be good! How is home? I miss you all so much. I stay with Auntie, and she is doing good. I am now a secretary to the Assistant Director of Medical Services. It breaks my heart to see how this war goes on and on. Thelma and I have to have our uniform hung up and ready all the while. You never know when you will be called for duty. If a troop ship comes in at two o'clock in the morning, then the military police will come to our home, knock on the door and in five minutes flat we have to be dressed to go down to the troop ship. It breaks my heart – you see fit young men leave all hale and hearty and you see them come back on stretchers; you see them come back in wheelchairs. No news yet from Charlie, Ben, Sammy or Michael. Every time I go down to meet a troop ship, my heart is in my throat that it will, or it won't, be my own brothers.

You are all always in my prayers. Enclosing our wages and all of my love.

Merry Christmas, God bless,

Leila

FACT FILE

SOMEWHERE TO LIVE

• •

Many white British people didn't want to rent rooms to Black people, even if they had a job, simply because of the colour of their skin. So, many Black people were forced to live in the worst areas. Landlords sometimes charged them more to live in unsafe, overcrowded places in areas that had been bombed out during the war. If they complained or missed paying their rent, when they came home from work they could find the landlord had thrown all their belongings out on the street. So, African-Caribbean people began joining together to save money to buy their own houses.

Claude Ramsey came to England from Barbados in 1956 on board the *Antilles*. His first home in England was a house in Notting Hill Gate. About thirty people lived in the house and they all had to share just one bath and one toilet. Later on he went to live with his brother in Paddington.

Isolyn Robinson came to England from Jamaica in 1954. She remembered: "My aunt had been here for three years with her husband and she found me a little room in her house in Geneva Road. It was so small I called it my Spoon Room. There was no inside toilet in the house and the only running water was a tap in the backyard." Isolyn saved money and eventually she managed to buy her own house.

Winston and Lynette Findlater, a couple from Jamaica, came to Britain on the *Empire Windrush*. Mrs Findlater had a hard time getting a job but when she did the hours were long and it wasn't well paid. However, she managed to save money towards a deposit for a house in South London.

• •

A man stands on a street, Notting Hill, 1961

MADE TO MEASURE

QUINCY THE COMEDIAN

Every young person has goals, dreams and ambitions. Mine was to become a tailor of suits. I'd dreamed of becoming a tailor since I was a boy in Barbados, watching movies fresh from the States and the UK at the cinema. Even more than the actors' costumes, I used to admire the clothes of the touring countries who played the West Indies cricket team; how smart they looked on and off the pitch. I thought to myself, *One day, I'm going to either play for the West Indies team or make their suits.*

Growing up, money wasn't flowing. We couldn't afford new clothes, but with the help of my mother, I always tried to make my school uniform look a little different from my classmates'. My mum was an expert with a needle and thread. She could make anything from curtains to bedspreads. At the local market, we'd wander up and down the rows hunting for fabrics. As I grew up, I came to recognize good-quality cloth off the back of what my mum taught me.

One time, when the West Indies was playing England, I asked a friend who worked for the club to sneak me into the cricket ground, not just to see my beloved West Indies but to get a closer look at the outfits of both teams. As the captains came on to the field for the toss, I admired their smart jackets, made of light material to keep them cool under the hot sun.

I was so passionate about becoming a tailor, when the opportunity came to go to England to work in a clothes factory, I knew I had to take it. My cousin Kevin already worked at the factory, making garments for English stores. When he wrote to my mother and mentioned his company were looking to recruit new workers, she saw what a brilliant chance this was for me. I was so excited to chase my dream of becoming a tailor, I would have left Barbados without packing my own clothes. My mother brought me back to reality, making long lists of all the things I'd need in England and stitching extra layers into my favourite shirts, so I wouldn't be too cold.

A few weeks later, I boarded a ship bound for England. I was fascinated by the stories of the other passengers. Some of them were travelling to be with family:

"The last time dat boy step foot in my house, he was so small. Couldn't read, write – nothing. Now he writing me letters!"

"My wife thinks I'm going to write once I get there. When she eventually reach – and Lord she going to reach – I'm just going to say, 'When me reach England all the pen and paper run out.'"

Some, like me, were following opportunities and starting new adventures. They were hoping to get jobs in transport or with the new National Health Service, which provided free healthcare for everyone. They hoped that, when they came back home, they could tell stories about what they had done to help the mother land.

When we arrived at the dock, I had to raise my jacket collar to combat the cold breeze whistling against my neck. My teeth were chattering and it was May – that couldn't be right! As soon as I could get hold of some heavy fabric, I would make some gloves, a hat and a scarf.

Once all the paperwork was filled out, I headed to the coach station to meet my cousin.

"Winston!" Kevin's voice called. We hugged each other, and I held on a second too long, trying to absorb some of the heat from his coat.

I'd never seen so many white people at once. I wondered why so many of them were staring at us. They were all smartly dressed and in a rush going who knows where. We got on a coach travelling to London. I looked out the window at the masses of green, thinking how many cricket games you could play here.

"Wake up! You want to get to the factory late? I've told the boss about you and first impressions count over here."

I blinked as Kevin's face swam into focus above me. I'd fallen asleep almost as soon as I'd got into my new room the night before. My cousin lived down the corridor, and we shared a kitchen and bathroom with lots of other people. I got out of bed and began putting on my clothes as quickly as possible – it was still so cold! Luckily, I'd kept my socks on overnight so at least my feet weren't freezing.

"What's the boss's name?" I asked.

"Mr Tardelli, he's Italian. Now, hurry up!"

On the bus I recognized the conductor's accent as he asked us for the fare – a fellow Barbadian! As we pulled up to the stop outside the factory, I saw a steady flow of workers clocking into the building.

I followed Kevin through the factory. There was fabric all around, all different colours, textures and patterns. The sound of hundreds of sewing machines rattled, and there was a radio playing in the background. I heard snippets of conversation from the workers scattered around the factory floor, as busy as elves working on Christmas Eve. I felt like I was in heaven (without the heating). This was the start of my journey to becoming a tailor.

Eventually, we arrived outside Mr Tardelli's office. Through the glass, I could see a small man speaking on the phone and smoking. He glanced up and beckoned us in.

"I've got to go now," he was saying loudly into the phone. "Just make sure I get what I order."

He turned to Kevin. "Sorry about that, business is business. How are you, my friend?"

My cousin and Mr Tardelli exchanged pleasantries, then Kevin introduced me.

"I've been told back home you are a bit of a dab hand at making clothes," said Mr Tardelli. I replied with a nod. "I've also been told you're a very hard worker, like your cousin here."

"Yes," I said. "I hope to become a tailor some day – I'd love to have my own shop and make clothes for famous people!"

This was met with a smile by the boss. "I like this one," he said, putting his arm around me. His cigarette smoke swirled around my face. "He's got ambition and dreams. Let's see how long it lasts when the English weather kicks in. We'll start you off pressing. I'll put you next to old John – he'll show you the ropes!"

I could see from John's face that I wasn't the first guy he'd shown the ropes. He had the words 'West Ham' tattooed on his knuckles.

"What team do you support?" he asked as I sat down at the workstation next to him.

"Team?"

"Team, mate – football." John peered at me suspiciously. "You do like football, right? Don't tell me – you're a cricket fan probably?"

I nodded and he sighed. "The ball's too small. The only thing I like about cricket is it's five days without seeing my missus."

"Football is ninety minutes though; shouldn't that give you more time to spend with your wife?" I replied cheekily. John laughed, and I felt relieved to have broken the ice.

"I like you, you're quick-witted. If you're as nice as your cousin says you are, I'll take you to see my beloved West Ham some day."

He started showing me how to press the finished garments. He was a good teacher, and I picked it up quickly. Around the factory floor, there were several large buckets filled with cloth. Every now and then, a worker tossed a piece of material into a bucket.

"What do you do with that fabric?" I asked John.

"It's scrap from what the cutting department doesn't use," he replied. "It gets chucked at the end of the week."

I was amazed at the amount of fabric being thrown away. As I caught the bus home that night, I kept thinking about all the things my mum could create with that unused material. It seemed a shame for it to go to waste…

Over the next few weeks, I settled into my new job at the factory. I soon built up the courage to ask Mr Tardelli about the scrap material. He didn't have a problem with me taking some of it home, so I saved up for my own sewing machine and mannequin and began to practise tailoring in my spare time. When the guys from the factory went to the pub after work, I honed my craft and tried to copy the suits I'd seen on the cinema screens back home, and on the famous cricketers, who I hoped to see play in England some day. It was hard work, but my dream of becoming a tailor drove me forward.

As the months went by, I gathered more fabric and learned to make everything from shirts to full three-piece suits. Soon, word spread that I could make clothes, and people were knocking on my door, asking me to make all kinds of things, from school uniforms to suits for special occasions. I became the go-to tailor for the Caribbean community. I was proud to send home a bit of extra money each time I wrote to my mum, telling her of my progress in England.

One day I got to work early and bumped into John who was snooping around my station.

"Have you lost something?" I asked, heading over.

"I came in early to drop off a ticket for you, to see West Ham against Fulham. You said you like to see the flash suits, didn't you? Well, that's

101

what the players wear before they start the game. Think of it as a leaving present."

"But I'm not leaving!" I said.

"No, you're not, I am," John replied. He told me his time at the factory was done and he had trained me well enough to continue the job. He was going to work with his son-in-law.

"Thanks for the ticket! But John, at your age, you should be retiring and relaxing!" I said.

John laughed and collected his hat and coat. "I'll retire soon, just gonna help out the son-in-law for a bit at his posh new shop and that's me finished. And when West Ham wins the FA Cup, I'll come to a cricket match with you."

"I'll buy you a ticket to a West Indies game some day," I told him. "Then you'll see what a real match is like."

We hugged, and I wished him the best for his team and the future.

"Take this card – it's for my son-in-law's shop. Anytime you want a nice suit, come and see him." John handed me a business card and I glanced at the address. Savile Row – all the fanciest tailors worked on that street! I put it in my wallet with a smile.

Time passed. I worked at the factory and made clothes in the evenings and at the weekends. I got an order for a wedding, to make suits for the groom, best man and ushers. It was a big job, which could earn me enough to get my own place, with room for my stock. As I was sewing one afternoon, Kevin walked in all excited.

"What you smiling for?" I asked.

"You see that girl I tell you about every day, who live down the street? Well, I catch a date."

"Where are you going to take her?"

"Not me, we. You always stuck in this room, like an elf making clothes. I told her to bring a friend and I'll bring you. A double date."

The news went through me like an electric bolt, so much so that I took my eye off my sewing machine and caught my hand. I yelped in pain. I knew my injury was bad when my cousin called the Lord's name. I lifted my hand to control the bleeding and Kevin picked up some scrap material and covered it.

At the hospital, they stitched up my cut, put on a bandage and told me I'd be out of action for a while. The news was devastating. I'd never be able to make those wedding suits now. And even working at the factory would be difficult.

Mr Tardelli wasn't best pleased and I was reduced to doing simple jobs around the factory. Even after my hand healed, I found it hard to build up business again. It seemed my dream of becoming a tailor, with my own shop and famous clients, would never come true.

I was pretty low, until one day I heard some exciting news. The West Indies cricket team was coming to England to tour in the summer! This was my opportunity to see my heroes outside of Barbados. I had enough money to buy a ticket instead of sneaking into the ground as I had back home. There was one person I wanted to take to the match with me.

I caught a bus to London's West End, gazing out the windows at the glittering buildings, so tall they almost touched the sky. I got to my destination and checked the address on the card I still kept in my wallet. The tidy row of shops, with their windows full of crisp shirts and smart suits, made me feel overwhelmed. I took off my hat and opened the door. The smell of fresh material washed over me as I stepped inside.

"Good afternoon, sir, can I help you?" a gentleman asked, hurrying over to me.

"Yes, I was given this card by a friend of mine who helped me when I first came to this country. His name is John – is he here by any chance?"

"You're not Winston, are you?" the gentleman asked. He broke into a smile when I nodded. "John was speaking about you last week. He said you might pop in one day."

He asked me to wait while he went out the back to fetch John. I looked around the shop, admiring the suits and matching shoes.

"It must cost an arm and a leg to buy in here," I muttered to myself. Far more than what I normally charged.

John came out through a door at the back of the shop with a tape measure around his neck.

"Winston!" he cried.

"I said I'd come and see you when the West Indies came over," I told him. "I'm going to show you how we celebrate cricket West Indian style. I've bought you a ticket – consider it a thank-you present, for helping me when I first arrived."

John replied with a wave of his hand. He introduced me to his son-in-law, Michael, the gentleman who had greeted me when I'd come into the shop and told him all about my dream of becoming a tailor. I mentioned my injury, and how I'd been finding it hard to get my business back up and running. The conversation flowed and at some points it felt like an interview. It was nice to hear about Michael's success.

"I'm actually opening up another shop soon. We've already got some famous clients booked in…" Michael told me. "What are your plans over the weekend? It's our grand opening."

The opening day came around and I dressed up in my finest attire. The new shop was just as stylish as the Savile Row store. John introduced me to his family and friends.

"I'd like to thank everyone for coming," Michael announced. "I hope to make this shop just as successful as the original. In every shop you need good staff and someone to manage those staff. Now, the person I have in mind doesn't know this yet, but I hope they'll take this opportunity to follow their dreams and run this new venture."

Michael called me over. I was confused but moved towards him. He leaned over to whisper in my ear. "I would love you to manage the shop, Winston."

I was overwhelmed but, before I could reply, it was projected across the room:

"Ladies and gentlemen, please welcome our new manager and wonderful tailor, Winston. And our first clients, the West Indies cricket team, will be coming in for a suit fitting tomorrow."

My emotions got the better of me as tears of joy flowed down my face. Every young person has goals and ambitions. Every young person has a dream – and mine was about to come true.

THE WIND AND THE SNOW

E.L. NORRY

Jayston liked Boxing Day almost as much as Christmas Day. After lunch, his younger cousins headed upstairs to play with Lego and it was finally time for Jayston to fire up the PlayStation. Aunty Rose had given him the latest FIFA game, and he couldn't wait to put in some serious hours with his mates from his old school online. His mum and aunts headed into the kitchen, laughing loudly. Soon tunes were blaring from the radio and dishes were clattering.

The living room was cosy, with the heating on full blast, and Jayston had a mouthful of fizzy cola bottles. Life didn't get much better than this.

Grandpa Victor stood by the window, his hand on the curtains, staring out across the driveway, sipping at his tea. "Get up and come look 'ere," he said.

Even though Grandpa Victor had come to Britain over seventy years ago, when he was twelve – the same age as Jayston now – he still carried a warm Jamaican accent. He was the only member of their family who had an accent and Jayston felt relaxed whenever he heard it.

"What's up?" Man United had just finished loading. He turned around in his gaming chair. "I'm about to start this Champions League final."

Jay was so happy to be off school for two weeks. Away from the pressure and that group of boys who'd said they didn't believe Jayston was mixed-race when he mentioned his grandpa and Jamaica in a classroom discussion. He'd never heard that rubbish back in Hackney, but there weren't many Black kids in this new school.

"Don you be cheeky." Grandpa Victor pulled at the net curtains. "Look at all de snow out dere. Ain't dat sometin'?"

Jay yawned. All that curry had made him sleepy. "It'll be mush in a minute. Mum says it won't settle – never does."

"I 'member when I first see snow…" Grandpa's voice was soft, his face loose and relaxed from the curried goat and sorrel tea that had been flowing.

Jayston barely glanced up from his controller. "No!" He spammed the X button to get off a good pass. "Foul! Get off!"

Grandpa Victor tutted. "Playing your silly games on dat box, staring into nothin', eyes so big … as if you doin' something important. Why don you help your mother in da kitchen?"

Jay rolled his eyes. *Really?* Grandpa just had no idea how hard Jayston had been working recently, how this was his chance to finally relax. Grandpa always said the same things: help your mother, do more chores, work hard. Jayston was bored of hearing it. Anyway, these days Mum preferred him to be indoors and not out on the estate, especially when it got dark so early.

Jay tried to explain. "Gramps… Mum's been missing her sisters. And I just got Rashford! This is *strategy*. If you knew how important this game was, what a battle, then you'd see I'm not just messing around—"

"Show me whas so important then!" Grandpa waved his hand at the other controller.

Was he serious? He wanted to play? Jayston reloaded the game for two players. He handed the controller to Grandpa and explained what the buttons did. "I'll go easy on you," he joked.

Grandpa laughed. "Don you worry about me, boy. You watch yourself…"

"You move your players with the stick." Jayston grinned at his Grandpa squinting at the screen as he brought a player down the wing.

"Your great-granddad, my father – he flew planes. He fought in a *real* war."

"Which one?"

"What dem teachers doin'? The Second World War!"

Jay thought about last term's history lessons. He didn't remember seeing any Black faces in the newspaper reports, or on the TV reels. They'd read about Indians at Dunkirk, but no one from the West Indies had been mentioned. If his Jamaican great-grandparents had fought for Britain, why hadn't Jay heard about it?

"I don't get it. What happened?"

"The British come over to Jamaica an' asked people to fight for their mother country. We was a colony, ruled by Britain then. Places in Jamaica named after places in England, schools taught British history. My father sang 'God Save the King' in school and learned all bout dem dead kings and queens. Strong men were needed to come over and fight. Thousands signed up. Didn't hesitate. *Thousands.*"

"We haven't been taught about that in history."

"Well, some of dem teachers don like to tell you too much about the tings those men did."

Grandpa pressed the square button and laughed as his ball went into the net. "Ha! Goal!"

"Beginner's luck!" Jayston said. He should pay closer attention – no need to go easy on Grandpa, was there?

Fighting in a war, for his country, wasn't something Jay had ever considered before, but now he did. What would he fight for, and who? After that trouble with the name-calling last term, his mum was right – violence didn't solve anything. She believed in marching, peaceful protests, signing petitions: standing up for what she thought was right and fair, just like her mother had.

"But if it wasn't really their country, why did they want to fight?" Jayston asked, neatly manoeuvring his player past Grandpa's.

"They felt like it was their country. That's the thing. An' they was proud, all dem young boys wanted to fight for King and Empire." Grandpa hunched forward, tongue slightly out of the corner of his mouth now as he was getting into the game.

Aunty Rose poked her head round the kitchen door. "You playing? Well, finish up, Pops, because we're heading off in about fifteen minutes. I want to get on to the M25 and home before dark." She closed the kitchen door and soon the laughing started up again.

"Home?" Grandpa had put down his controller and stopped playing. "Seventy-two years me been 'ere. This me home. But some of what de people yell at me? 'Go back to where ya came from!' Me was so confused. 'Go home'? I was home."

Jayston hadn't heard Grandpa talk much about when he first came over here. But lately, since the Windrush scandal had been more in the news, it seemed that the past was playing on his mind.

Jayston knew a little about the *Empire Windrush*. A famous boat that had brought people from the West Indies in 1943. Grandpa was one of the first ones here. Over the years, more and more boats had brought people from the West Indies and other places, who'd chosen to make Britain their home.

Grandpa sucked his teeth, which is what he did when he was getting vexed.

"Seems we was good enough to make Britain a great nation, but not good enough to be given a roof over our heads. Turned away … door after door. Then dem signs goin' up: *no coloureds*."

Jay blanched. No coloureds. You couldn't say that! Heat rushed into his cheeks as he remembered those kids telling him he couldn't be Black just because he was so light-skinned. How that had made him feel; like half of him didn't exist. It made him feel strange; he wondered what difference the colour of his skin made to who he was, and how he felt, inside.

"People … they'd just say that? Openly? On signs?" Jay knew all about

Malcolm X and the race troubles in America, but had that stuff happened over here too?

Grandpa Victor went back over to the window, looking outside.

"Ach. Me couldn't even learn in school in peace, gettin' called names. Teachers thinkin' we stupid and putting us in with younger kids. But me keep me mouth shut an' me head down. That's what you did. Give no trouble and cha get no trouble..." His words trailed off.

He put on his overcoat. "We do all dat for dem and den dey turn roun – all dis Windrush nonsense – and tell us go home? That we don belong... That we need our papers... Me come here on me mudda's passport, me tole me not need me own."

"That's not fair!" Jay cried. How dare they treat his granddad like that!

His grandpa smiled, but it was a sad smile. "Dat's true boy, but whas fair for some, don come into it for others."

"Did your dad even like it here?"

"My father... He tell me only once about him arriving, seeing dem chimneys – thought them was factories. He din know people was so cold they needed fires in their houses! They treat him good in the war, but after... He came home to us in St Catherine. An' a few years later, Britain need our help again. Posters all over. Not to fight dis time, but to rebuild. Them hospitals and schools weren't gunna build demselves. Thousands were dead an' Britain was in pieces."

Grandpa looked deep into Jayston's eyes. "Sometimes he say how much he miss his family; the beaches. The palm trees. The sun. You should visit one time. See for yerself."

Grandpa ruffled Jay's curls. "You an' Mum all settled here now? You feel dis is home?"

Was Poole home? Jayston was born in Hackney, and that's where Grandpa and his aunts and cousins still lived. Jayston had already moved twice: first, the divorce, and then Mum's new job. Sometimes he felt like those hermit crabs, lining up to share shells in a conga line. But he liked it down here, near the sea, and last summer he learned to surf.

He shrugged. "Yeah, I suppose."

Grandpa Victor shook his head and his eyes went a little misty. "Home ain't jus where you live. Home is your heart an yer history. An history ain't just what they tell you neither. You got to look beyond the books. You got to speak to people. They was promised tings: jobs, money. They was tole Britain was this wunnerful place…"

"Who'd want to come here if they had sunshine and beaches?"

"Understan, there was no work. You can't live off mangos! The '44 hurricane ruined the houses, the crops. When your great-granddad got back to St Catherine – there was nothin' for him. He thought we have a better life here, so he bring us over. I was so sick on that boat, took a month! Believe! All dem waves crashing, my stomach rolling. Even tho me from an island, me never like da water after that."

Jayston couldn't imagine being on a boat for that long, staring out at nothing but ocean. He stood next to his grandpa and looked out of the window too. The snow looked peaceful.

"You gunna be tall," Grandpa said, smiling. "You'll be turning away all dem ladies." He put his arm loosely around Jayston's shoulder and squeezed.

"Gramps …" Jayston blushed, but hoped Grandpa was right. Now he was just a bunch of long limbs and bony elbows, teased about his frizzy hair and full lips.

"Love save me, ya know. I didn't feel on me own no more. Life really start wen I met your Gramma. She got trouble for stepping out with me, but we was in love."

"What happened?"

"She tole her parents, but they wasna listening. They say for her not to come back home. She was brave. Weren't the thing, to be seen with a Black man in dem days. She got spat at, called names. She come to my work one day, I see her lickle suitcase and she say, 'I'm here now. You wamme or not?' Fifty-five years ago…"

Jayston didn't remember his grandma; she'd died when he was only three. But Mum and her two sisters often toasted her memory – remembering her passion for fighting injustice by going on marches, and making placards.

"Let us step outside. Me want to see wimme own eyes the snow."

Grandpa opened the front door and Jay followed. He laughed and shivered as the cold air blasted through. A dusting of snow fluttered on the doorstep.

Jay looked at the parked cars across the road, the windscreens all white.

"When I see snow dat first time … it make everything so quiet. It stopped alla noise. I heard everything, the world even – all crisp. My parents were sleeping. We was crammed in one room. I stood on the doorstep at six o'clock in the mornin'. There was this light, this brightness to the world that I ain't never seen before, not here anyway – all white, and perfect and clean. Like God was givin' me a present. Showin' me jus how lovely this place could be. No more dirt, no more grey … and it seemed like a sorta sign. Of all the good things that could come to us. Even if, right then, we was jus in one lickle room. It wouldn't always be like dat."

Jay looked up at his Grandpa's lined face and the dancing sparkle in his brown eyes as he smiled at the memory. It was beautiful.

"All de people that come, that left their beautiful island – they jus wan a new life, ya know? A better one for dem and their children. We worked hard. Work makes you respec' yourself. You gotta work hard. Your gramma, she do the nursing, caring and helpin' people. You got to be part of something bigger than youself, you unnerstan? That's what you got to do. Find that thing to be a part of. And then… Well then, no one can tell you that you don belong."

Jayston stepped on to the front step and held out his hands. Snowflakes dropped into his palm and, as quickly as they landed, they melted into nothingness. He stared right up into the sky and felt the snow on his cheeks, tiny darts of freshness.

A snowflake fizzed on his palm: pink and brown. He turned his hand over: brown and pink. He turned his hand over and over.

It wouldn't always be like this.

FACT FILE

THE WINDRUSH GENERATION

· ·

When the Windrush generation began to arrive in Britain they were surprised that white British people didn't know much about them although they came from countries that were a part of the British Empire. In the Caribbean, Britain claimed island colonies like Jamaica as well as islands in the Atlantic like Barbados and Bermuda. Britain also claimed one colony in South America called British Guiana (today's Guyana) and a colony in Central America called British Honduras (today's Belize). Some of the Caribbean people who came to Britain in the 1950s and 1960s were of Asian descent but most were of African ancestry.

The Windrush generation refers to the African-Caribbean people who came to Britain from the Caribbean. However, Africans also came and, being Black as well, they experienced the same treatment as the Windrush generation. You can read about this in the story 'Eliza King is at Home' on page 45.

Some of the Windrush generation settlers were writers, poets, musicians and artists. George Lamming and Samuel Selvon were good friends who came to England together from Trinidad in 1950. George was of African descent while Sam was of Indian descent. They both wrote books about the experiences of Black people coming to Britain from the Caribbean. E.R. Braithwaite from British Guiana helped Britain during the war. He later became a teacher. He wrote a story about his experiences called *To Sir, With Love*, which was later made into a movie.

· ·

Guyanese-born writer Edward Ricardo Braithwaite, circa 1960

Barbadian-born writer and poet George Lamming in London, 1951

GREEN ANGEL

JUDY HEPBURN

I'm eighteen years old and the Swinging Sixties are just beginning. There are clothes in the shops that I want to buy, neat suede jackets with no collars and colourful silk scarves for your neck instead of ties. And music! There's music everywhere. You still have to be careful walking home at night, in case you bump into the last of the Teddy Boys who think it's fun to chase lone Black men, sometimes just to scare us or sometimes worse.

I left school at fourteen and started working at Hartley's Jam Preserves, based in Southwark, just down the road. I've clocked in and out five days a week for four years. I enjoy having the money. It comes sealed up in a little brown envelope; some notes and coins, with a handwritten piece of paper making a note of how much I earned that week, if there was any overtime, and how much the government takes in income tax. I give some money to my mum and dad and the rest is mine. These days I find myself wondering about my future. I know I don't want to stay at the jam factory for much longer.

Mum and Dad always arrange things so they get a few days off together in the summer and we go on family trips. For three years straight we've gone to Margate.

"Margate again?" I ask, as the holidays come round.

"What's wrong with Margate?" my dad replies.

We set off early on a Saturday morning, catching the train from London Victoria. Margate station is very close to the sea and, even though it's our third year going to the same place, my heart leaps at the sight of the waves rolling lazily on to the shore. It reminds me of my journey to England and connects me to my granny. I haven't seen her since I left Jamaica as a small boy.

We always stay at the same little hotel in Margate, not too far from the seafront. After breakfast I usually go to the end of the pier and spend the day there, looking out to sea and daydreaming, while Mum, Dad and my brother, Trevor, sit on the beach behind a wind break drinking cups of tea from a flask. There's no getting away from it. I never settled down in London. I love my family, but those early years they spent together without me keep us apart.

"Stay with us this morning for once," my mother says as I get up to go.

"Leave the boy alone," I hear Dad saying. "He's thinking."

Today, instead of walking to the end of the pier, I explore the Penny Arcade. After playing the machines for a little I spot a booth with a sign outside that says a clairvoyant will read your future in the palm of your hands, for two and six. I sit and wait, squashing up on a row of chairs with some older ladies wearing headscarves.

When it's my turn I get up and go into the next room. I can't help smiling, for a young woman, probably a little older than me, sits there with gold hoop earrings and dark hair cut straight across her forehead, hiding her powder blue eyes. She seems surprised to see me too because we look at each other before she waves her hand for me to sit down.

"Cross my palm with silver then."

I'm puzzled.

"Show us your money," she says, in a northern accent.

"Oh. Right," I say, coughing up my two and six and holding out my hands, palm up.

I'm not really listening to what she says until, "You're going to have fish and chips later today, in a bus shelter on the promenade."

"I am?"

"You are. With a young lady from Leeds."

"Does she have a fringe by any chance?" I say.

"She does."

"And what time will this be?"

"Five o'clock."

"Rock or Cod?"

"Cod."

And so we have our first date, Mary and me, getting our fingers greasy, swapping our life stories.

We spend all our time together after that. When the summer season closes I visit her in Leeds and meet her parents. Leeds is about as far away from the sea as you can get, but it does have the Yorkshire Moors on its doorstep and I love the wildness of those hills and the greenness of the valleys. I am amazed to see all the stars. I haven't seen so many since my boyhood years in the Jamaican countryside. They bring a lump to my throat.

No matter how hard we try I just don't seem to fit in with my family in London; I don't seem to belong.

But with Mary, I feel at home.

She gets some stick for marrying a Black man. Not from her family, thank goodness, but from friends and strangers. She begs me not to leap to her defence if someone calls her names on the street.

"Water off a duck's back," she says, "it's not worth it, love, you'd be forever fighting."

It takes a while to get a job in Leeds as, every time I try to get one, I'm told that the vacancy was filled. Eventually, though, I get a job in a factory as a sheet-metal worker. We make all sorts of things, including parts for the Ginetta racing cars factory, just outside the city. I get involved with the trade union and go to night school, studying how to make the workplace fairer. I become a senior shop steward for the union and am proud of that. Things need to change and I want to play my part.

Once the children start arriving, I work nights – the pay is better and I get to spend more time with them.

"How do you fancy being a photographer?" Mary's father asks me on my thirtieth birthday, handing over his old camera.

I get quite good at taking pictures. There is a fairly large West Indian community in Leeds now so West Indian weddings become a sideline. I turn the cellar of the house into my darkroom. Then I get asked to take some pictures at a funeral, then a fiftieth wedding anniversary and then so many events start coming in I am working weekends too. One day, I look at the latest batch of photos strung up like washing on a line, and realize I am documenting something new, bigger than me – a glimpse of the Black community in post-war Britain. I begin taking photos in earnest, not waiting to be asked but making a record of our lives.

There isn't a lot of interest in my work but I know it's a good archive and sooner or later it will help people to see us and the part we played in helping to build Britain after the Second World War.

These days, life is pretty quiet. All four of our children have grown up. The girls have gone into nursing, office work and teaching and my son is a bus driver. Two of them have got families of their own now.

Mary and I sold up when I retired and we bought a smaller house on the outskirts of Leeds, in a village called Marsden. Village life means a smaller house, as it's just the two of us now, but a bigger garden, which we love. We grow our own vegetables and I've made a large wire cage for a chicken coop at the end. The chickens have plenty of room to scratch and peck and roost in some low branches and it serves to keep the foxes out.

Packing up took a month, there was lots to throw away and so many things to stop and stare at, as we sifted through the years. I came across some old Manila envelopes full of curled-up photographs that never made it into the photo albums, begun by Mary when we got married.

This afternoon, I'm sitting on the floor in our new house wondering what to do with them all, when one of them grabs my attention. I can make out three people. Me, about five years old, looking criss – nice and smart – in my white shirt and bow-tie, short trousers, socks and Clarks shoes standing on the side of a road. That photograph, I now understand, was a testament for my mother to see that the money she sent for her son got spent on her son.

My tall, thin granny is beside me in her Sunday dress. You can't tell from the photograph as it's faded now, and had been hand-tinted anyway, but that dress was a deep turquoise and her emerald green pillbox hat had a short veil, in the same colour, pushed back for the photo. She towers over the wiry frame of my grandpa in his suit. I only remember him in a singlet vest, patched trousers rolled to his knee, water boots and a faded red shirt flapping open, a machete in his right hand.

That machete was the only tool he needed. It chopped back the invading bush, dug holes in the earth for seedlings to nestle into, cut tender stems for grafting. It hung at his waist during the day when it was idle and spent the night on the floor under his bed.

I get up and look out of the window, my mind's eye not seeing the rolling green hills of England but the rich red earth of my Jamaican mountainside. When the kids in my English school called me names I saw my granny in her emerald green hat, the veil framing her dark face like a halo, throwing cracked rice on the ground for the hens clucking around her feet. When I wrapped two scarves around my neck and opened the front door to icy rain in the morning dark, when I bared my teeth in a pretend smile at some wisecrack at work about the colour of my skin, my granny was there, forever in my heart, even though she passed a long time ago.

Mary enters the room and walks over to me. Her once dark hair is white now. She rests her head on my shoulder. I put my arm around her waist. I know my granny would love her and be proud of how I've lived my life.

FACT FILE

THE WINDRUSH SCANDAL

In 2018 many people in Britain learnt from the media about the 'Windrush scandal'. The Home Office (a part of the government that deals with issues like immigration, passports and visas) wrongly told many Black British people that they should not be in Britain. Because of this mistake some people lost their jobs and homes, couldn't get health care and were wrongly deported.

This was called the 'Windrush Scandal' because those affected were some of the children of the Windrush generation. When the Windrush generation came to Britain from the Caribbean, those countries were still a part of the British Empire. In those days their birth certificates, passports and other documents just said that a person was a 'British Subject' (someone who was born in the United Kingdom or any of its colonies). Legally the Windrush generation were not immigrants. Because they came from Britain's colonies, their nationality was the same as white British people.

Later on the British Empire broke up and countries became independent from Britain. However, people who came to live in Britain before independence were still British. The staff in the Home Office forgot this important part of British history and thousands of people had their lives badly affected as a result. Now the government has to work to try to make things right again and to make sure their staff understand British history.

Walter Lothen came to Britain from Jamaica in 1954. At that time Jamaica was still a part of the British Empire. He remembers: "People did think

England was the mother country. When I came here I didn't have a status as a Jamaican. I was British and going to the mother country was like going from one parish [in Jamaica] to another. You had no conception of it being different."

A group of protesters gather outside Downing Street, London to mark the first official Windrush Day with a demonstration demanding justice for members of the Windrush generation, 22 June 2019

MAKING FRIENDS THE BRITISH WAY: LUCILLE'S STORY

KATY MASSEY

This book, *Coming to England*, is how I have survived my first six weeks in Hackney. But there is one problem it can't help with. How do the English make friends?

According to my book, they don't. It tells it like this:

The way people live here, you can be in the same house for years and never share a word with the other tenants. Respect that privacy. People don't ask their neighbours for a dust of salt here. They don't stand up on the doorstep gossiping, or form a crowd on the pavement to talk. What they like is politeness.

It seems this was one problem I would have to solve myself.

Here in London there are eight million people, more souls than on the whole of Jamaica, but there is no one for me to talk to. My husband, Earnest, doesn't have this problem: driving his bus means he talks to people as they get on and off, and he has the men he works with to chat to back at the bus station. But I'm alone all day, at least until I can get a job.

I used to think British people would be like my family in Port Royal. In Jamaica, I chatted to everyone all the time: to the old man at the roadside stall selling hairy yams and mangos as red as a baby's backside, to the ladies at church about the minister's sermon and, of course, we all talked about the people rebuilding their homes after the great hurricane of '44. Everyone knew everyone and all their business. Now I've arrived in England, I know that the British are not friendly like us, even though I learned in school that the Empire is supposed to be one big family.

Earnest found this room through one of the men he works with. His hours on the buses are long, which leaves the making of a home to me. *Coming to England* has told me everything practical. How to queue properly, how to put coins in the electricity meter, how not to cause offence. But it hasn't told me how to make friends. Or just a friend. Even one would do. I am so lonely here.

This adventure really began when I met Earnest at church and we started walking out together. At first we just smiled at each other, done up in our Sunday best. Then we started meeting up after service, going for walks and talking away. In Jamaica, I lived with my parents and worked for the British Army as a medical secretary. I started during the Second World War, when the Empire needed men to fight. I was used to the British recruiters coming to look for young men who were willing to join up. They searched every nook and cranny to find volunteers. I saw lots of healthy young men leave on the boats to fight. In fact, over the six years of the war, ten thousand went. But working in the army, I saw them come back too. They looked like ghosts of themselves; beautiful brown skin turned the colour of ashes in the grate. Their woollen uniforms hung off their shoulders as if they'd been made for bigger men. Some didn't have their full number of arms or legs. I was a medical secretary, so I got used to typing the details of their many injuries.

One afternoon, when I was walking with Earnest after church, I told him that I didn't understand why they went in the first place. "Especially as no one makes them do it," I said. "English boys, well, they have to go, but not ours."

But Earnest, who worked as a tailor in Kingston, saw it differently. "It's our mother country. And when your mother's in trouble, you gotta come."

"But no mother who loved her children would send them home in this state," I told him.

"But you're only seeing the ones who do come back. My uncle and his cousin will never come back here, except to visit. They call England 'the land of opportunity'."

I knew he loved their letters. He read – no – he drank every word in like a thirsty man. And he read and reread each one until it tore at the creases.

"There are plenty of jobs there, more than here anyway," Earnest added

Plenty of parties and pretty girls too! I thought, but I didn't say this. Instead I said: "Ha! The opportunity to freeze to death!"

But he didn't hear me. His eyes had drifted away from mine, to an invisible point far out to sea and way beyond Port Royal's small horizon. As the Sunday afternoon sky clouded over, I realized with a heavy heart that he was determined to join his family in England. Suddenly he turned and looked at me, a serious expression in his light brown eyes.

"Will you come with me, Lucille? Make a new life for us? And marry me, of course!"

I hesitated for only a few seconds.

"I'd be honoured to, Earnest Brownlow Junior!"

He threw his arms around me, and in that moment I was so happy. But I felt a little sadness too. Because I knew that I had promised to leave my parents and my friends to travel far away from home. But Earnest's face was so full of joy and love that I pushed my worries away. As we hugged, a tropical rain began falling. As the fat, warm drops soaked our faces, I didn't know if the sky cried, or I.

We married just two weeks later. Earnest left for England first, to get us established. After a year, I followed him. I looked forward to the journey, but dreaded it too. Leaving the island I loved to sail to another one I didn't know was bittersweet for me. My sea voyage to England felt like a very long three weeks, as I was sick nearly every day. I was overjoyed to see Earnest's smile at Southampton Docks. But as our train pulled towards London I was shocked. I only saw greyness and smoke, and dirty black brick and stone everywhere. It lay in great piles of rubble where Earnest told me German bombs had fallen. Worse, the smoke that belched from every chimney made the air so thick with soot that it was difficult to breathe.

When I saw our new home, I had another shock. Earnest has rented a bed-sitting room for us in Hackney. All the rooms in the house, all six of them, share one bathroom. And there's no maid here to do the cooking and cleaning either. At home, I didn't even fill my own bath, never mind share one.

My time to use the bath is on Thursday evenings, between seven o'clock and eight o'clock. This is my sixth week here and my sixth turn with the bath, but I'll never get used to it. I find the bathroom empty, but dirty, so as usual, I set to cleaning the bath first. Then I turn on the hot tap, but the water is icy cold. Half an hour later it is still cold. There is a sort of boiler thing on the wall. It spits gas and flames into the air as usual, but it doesn't heat the water at all.

I must have forgotten to shut the bathroom door properly because, as I struggle with the tap, the girl from downstairs appears on the landing behind me. I have seen her before, she's a blonde slip of a thing, and we have smiled but never talked. She must have heard me cursing and come to see what the fuss was about. *Coming to England* says not making a fuss is important here and I'm mortified. But at least I'm fully dressed! Anyway it's too late now, I can't shut the door in her face.

"Can I help you?" She speaks to me kindly, but so quietly she wouldn't wake a snake if it was sleeping under her chair.

"I can't heat the water. Heck! Everything is so hard here. Now I can't even have a bath!" This all comes out in a rush, and a curse slips out too. I couldn't help it.

"Oh, the boiler doesn't work very well. But there's a tank in the airing cupboard. It heats the hot water, but someone must have used it all. You'll have to wait for it to heat up again. Don't keep running the hot tap though. You have to give it a chance."

"That's what my Earnest says: 'Give it a chance, Lucille!' But I tell you, I've just about had enough!" I can't manage to be calm and polite tonight. I feel tears scratching the back of my eyes. "I'm sorry. I'm not going to cry…" But I can't help a sob escaping.

"Would you like to come to my room for a cup of tea?"

She smiles a lovely warm smile, such as I haven't seen for six weeks. Her small white teeth, and blonde bobbed hair, well, they make her look like the sun. And, as for tea, I can't think of anything I want more.

"But what about the person who's next in the bathroom? I'll lose my turn!"

"Don't worry about that. It's me next!"

She laughs and I join in, following her down the narrow stairs to her room.

Her room is exactly like ours except that, with just a single bed, it feels larger. I stand until she gestures for me to sit on the single wooden chair, while she fills a kettle and puts it on the hotplate. With her colourful bedspread and posters of Perry Como, Alma Cogan and Frankie Laine, it's a much more cheerful room than ours. I think that I should be a better wife to Earnest – try harder to make our own room feel like home – and the thought makes me want to cry again.

"So, how long have you been in Hackney?" asks the girl. "I can tell it's not been long enough to get used to our terrible plumbing!"

"I came six weeks ago. I didn't want to come, to tell you the truth. I had a good life in Jamaica."

"I'm sure you did," she says steadily, but she doesn't sound very sure of me. We both pause and she looks at me as if taking me in for the first time. I worry about my hair. Since I arrived in London I've had to start styling it myself. I set it on big curlers to stretch out the frizz, but at this rate, I'm not even going to get to wash it this week. I don't want her to think I'm showing off about my life in Jamaica. So, I try again.

"What's your name?" I ask her. "Mine's Lucille. But I think I already said that." I grin and hold out my hand. She puts down a cup of tea and a saucer in front of me, made with milk, not lemon like we drink it at home, but I decide not to mind.

"I'm Samantha. Nice to meet you!" She puts her small cool hand in mine and smiles back at me. I pump her arm so hard, she must think I'm trying to get water from a dry well.

"Whereabouts in Jamaica did you live?" Samantha asks, sitting on the edge of her bed.

"I lived with my family in Port Royal. Our small town lies a little way from Kingston, but it's quiet and peaceful, not like the capital with all its hustle and bustle," I reply, trying my best to act like the young woman my mother brought me up to be.

"I think I've heard the name…"

"Port Royal is famous because hundreds of years ago, during the time of slavery, it was known as the place where the pirates and privateers lived it up with their rum and suchlike…"

After that, Samantha tells me all about where she is from. It's somewhere called Coventry, which she says had a very hard time in the war and suffered a lot of bombing. I tell her about the hurricane of 1944, and our chatter becomes easy and familiar. She makes us more tea. After a while, I tell her how much I like the changes she has made to her room. Samantha says perhaps we could go shopping together and she could help me pick out some decorations for ours.

And just like that I have made a friend! Only one, but one friend is more than a hundred per cent better than no friends at all. All because of having to share a bathroom! But Earnest will also tell me it is because I finally learned to swallow my pride and accept help. A little later, we have finished our second cup of tea, and my comical story about the voyage to England makes my new friend laugh. I relax into Samantha's company and realize that I feel a hundred per cent happier about my new home too. The sound of us giggling together is sweet on my ear, and I look forward to hearing more of it. Like the music in our church in Jamaica, or the rustle of the trade wind blowing through the Hibiscus trees, our laughter, and her friendship, make this house feel like home at last.

ABOUT THE AUTHORS

K.N. CHIMBIRI

• •

"My parents came to Britain in the 1960s from Barbados. My dad worked as a conductor on the buses. Later on, he worked for the post office. My mum's first job was working for the Lyons chain of canteens and tea shops. These stories of the Windrush generation are an important part of modern British history. I am delighted to contribute to this wonderful book which remembers this era."

Kandace Chimbiri is the author of Black history books for children. Kandace is motivated by a desire to help improve both children's literacy as well as their knowledge of history.

KEVIN GEORGE

• •

"My mother's side of the family are from St Vincent and the Grenadines, and my father's side of the family are from Jamaica. My grandparents on both sides arrived in England in the early 1960s: cooking in the hospital, caring in a nursing home, making chocolate in the Cadbury factory, making metal in a gas factory and coil-winding. I found listening to the BCA audio documentaries and being given the opportunity to write 'The Light at the End of the Tunnel', a privilege. The stories of those that came to support England during and after the war are an important part of history and understanding the experience of Black people in England to this day."

Kevin George is a clinical consultant who delivers mental health and emotional literacy programmes to groups. He is the author of Soccology and a former professional football player.

SALENA GODDEN

· ·

"My family come from Jamaica. Like so many others, my grandparents left their home to come to the UK and they arrived on a boat to join the war effort. It is important to me that this sacrifice and their life stories are treasured and shared. It is an honour to be asked to be part of this book to keep this life alive!"

Salena Godden is a high-profile poet. She is also an author, broadcaster, essayist and memoirist whose work has been widely anthologized.

JUDY HEPBURN

· ·

"Listening to the oral histories of people who came to Britain after the Second World War is both an inspirational and humbling experience. My parents left Jamaica in 1947. They didn't come to England but in the late 1950s, as little girls, they sent my sister and me to school there. I am thankful and honoured to be a part of this anthology which will become part of the record of the cultural history of all these islands, on both sides of the Atlantic."

Judy Hepburn is a playwright and actress. A Jamaican brought up in the Malaysian state of Sarawak, Judy was sent to an English boarding school and lives in London.

ASHLEY HICKSON-LOVENCE

· ·

"My family on my mother's side are from St Lucia, and from Grenada on my dad's. My grandparents arrived in the UK from the West Indies between the late 1950s and the early 1970s and went on to be dinner ladies, carers, car mechanics and even lollipop men. It's so important that we continue to explore the stories of people who came to make new lives for themselves thousands of miles from their home and play their part in helping the mother country recover after the destruction of the Second World War."

Ashley Hickson-Lovence is a novelist and former schoolteacher who is currently completing his Creative Writing PhD at university writing about the life of a Black football referee from Jamaica.

JERMAIN JACKMAN

"The Windrush Scandal has shown us the importance in learning, understanding and acknowledging the contributions made by the Windrush generation to our country. The Windrush story reflects the story of so many others who moved to Britain in search of a better life. It's the story of my parents and granny. I would not be here, writing this, if it wasn't for their bravery so this is paying homage to them and my grandmother, Baby G."

Jermain Jackman is a singer, writer and activist who won The Voice UK in 2014.

KIRSTY LATOYA

"I grew up in a very Jamaican household around my very Jamaican family and I loved it! I was always in awe of the stories I was told about how each of them arrived in the UK, as every story was completely different. My mum was dropped off in the countryside to a family friend, armed with just a small bag of clothes and a hunger to survive. She went on to raise a family and become a nurse, carer, baker and even a church deacon. Exploring and understanding the Windrush generation is so important, these brave people stepped into the unknown and so many thrived despite adversity."

Kirsty Latoya is an illustrator and poet who explores important themes such as mental health, identity, womanhood and masculinity through her creations. She is an activist, and author of art and poetry book Reflections of Me.

KATY MASSEY

"I was so pleased to be asked to write Lucille's and Eliza's stories. People of colour – including my own family – have managed to settle into British society over many centuries. Though it hasn't always been easy, kinship and compassion were key to this success. While the contribution made by people of colour to London's place as one of the world's leading modern cities is a story is still being written, the kindness experienced and exhibited by Lucille and Eliza shows how numerous nationalities and religions have managed to live together peacefully and in friendship. It was a joy to give voice to these two vibrant, confident and resourceful women."

Katy Massey was a journalist for fifteen years before returning to university and beginning to write creatively. Her life writing and fiction has been shortlisted for several prizes.

E.L. NORRY

"I was born in Cardiff, Wales. Unfortunately, I don't know much about my father's family, which is the Jamaican side. We think my grandparents came to Wales from the Caribbean in the 50s or 60s. There was a lot of work down the mines and at the docks. Apparently, my father's parents were doctors or nurses, so they may have responded to the recruitment campaigns that ran throughout the Caribbean, as well as Malaysia and Mauritius. The NHS, like a lot of post-war Britain, was built by migrants. The Windrush generation, and their descendants are an important part of history and their contributions should not be forgotten."

E.L. Norry writes for both adults and children, and has a particular interest in exploring difficult issues and complex characters in a realistic, contemporary and accessible style.

QUINCY THE COMEDIAN

"Both of my parents are from Barbados. Growing up I experienced so many Barbadian sayings and phrases. Being that child whose trousers were bought too long. At the time I didn't understand why. But every school term I see that long queue outside the school uniform shop. Hence the making, and in my case, unravelling."

Award-winning comedian Quincy, also known as the Cockney Prince, is a stand-up comic and radio talk show host.

INDEX

PICTURE CREDITS

Every effort has been made to ensure that this information is correct at the time of going to print. Any errors will be corrected upon reprint.